Re

SOCIAL WORK AND CRIMINAL JUSTICE:

VOLUME 4

THE IMPACT OF THE POLICY ON SENTENCER DECISION MAKING

Louise Brow

Liz Levy

The Scottish Office Central Research Unit

THE SCOTTISH OFFICE CENTRAL RESEARCH UNIT
1998

Book No. **04299085**

30121 0 04299085

ACKNOWLEDGEMENTS

We are indebted to all those who kindly sacrificed a considerable amount of time out of their busy schedules to provide the researchers with their views: sheriffs; procurators fiscal; court social workers; and social workers.

We are also grateful to the police, social work departments, the Scottish Criminal Records Office and the Scottish Home Department criminal statistics for providing access to data and supplying information requested by the researchers.

We would also like to thank Mrs Helen Pinkman and Ms Mariane McGowan of the Central Research Unit for their patience in deciphering and typing the various drafts of the reports.

Louise Brown
Liz Levy
1998

Law
17 APR 1998
(IWK)
344.0313

© Crown Copyright 1998

The views expressed in this report are those of the
researcher and do not necessarily represent those of the
Department, the Secretary of State for Scotland or The Stationery Office.

SOCIAL WORK AND CRIMINAL JUSTICE
RESEARCH PROGRAMME REPORTS

Paterson, F. and Tombs, J. (1998)

Social Work and Criminal Justice: Volume 1 - *The Impact of Policy.* The Stationery Office.

Phase One:

McAra, L. (1998)

Social Work and Criminal Justice: Volume 2 - *Early Arrangements.* The Stationery Office.

Phase Two:

Brown, L., Levy, L. and McIvor, G. (1998)

Social Work and Criminal Justice: Volume 3 - *The National and Local Context.* The Stationery Office.

Brown, L., Levy, L. (1998)

Social Work and Criminal Justice: Volume 4 - *Sentencer Decision Making.* The Stationery Office.

McAra, L. (1998a)

Social Work and Criminal Justice: Volume 5 - *Parole Board Decision Making.* The Stationery Office.

McIvor, G. and Barry, M. (1998)

Social Work and Criminal Justice: Volume 6 - *Probation.* The Stationery Office.

McIvor, G. and Barry, M. (1998a)

Social Work and Criminal Justice: Volume 7 - *Community Based Throughcare.* The Stationery Office.

04299085

STAFFORDSHIRE
UNIVERSITY
LIBRARY

CONTENTS

Page No.

SUMMARY   vii

Chapter 1:   Background to the Study   1

Chapter 2:   Social Work Services and
                    Organisational Structures   5

Chapter 3:   Factors which influence Sentencer
                    Decision Making   13

Chapter 4:   Information provided in the
                    Social Enquiry Report   17

Chapter 5:   Sentencing Decisions   27

Chapter 6:   Impact of the Policy on
                    Sentencing Decisions   37

Annex I: National Standards: Objectives of
                    Social Work Practice   39

Annex II: Methodological Issues   40

Annex III: Sentencing Trends   42

References   46

STAFFORDSHIRE
UNIVERSITY
LIBRARY

SUMMARY

INTRODUCTION

The Policy

In Scotland, statutory social work services to offenders and their families are provided by the local authority social work departments. Since April 1991, the Scottish Office has reimbursed to social work departments the full costs of providing a range of statutory social work services in the criminal justice system. National Objectives and Standards (the National Standards) were introduced by the Social Work Services Group of the Scottish Office to coincide with the introduction of the 100 per cent funding initiative.

The National Standards and the 100 per cent funding initiative cover: social enquiry reports; court social work services; probation; community service; and community based throughcare (social work in prisons is funded by the Scottish Prison Service). Since 1991, the initiative has been extended to supervised release orders, bail information and accommodation schemes, and supervised attendance order schemes (the latter two schemes are not yet available on a national basis).

The main aims of the Government's policy are:

- to reduce the use of custody by increasing the availability, improving the quality and targeting the use of community based court disposals and throughcare services on those most at risk of custody, especially young adult repeat offenders;

- to enable offenders to address their offending behaviour and make a successful adjustment to law abiding life.

Background to the Research

Central Government's review and evaluation of implementation of the funding initiative and the National Standards involves a programme of inspection by Social Work Services Inspectorate (SWSI), interpretation of statistics and a programme of research.

The research programme examines progress towards policy objectives. Four sheriff court areas, each in separate social work authorities, were selected as study sites for Phase Two of the research programme to reflect areas of both high and low population density and to represent both specialist and more generic forms of organising social work criminal justice services. The names of the four areas have been anonymised in reports and are referred to as Scott, Wallace, Burns and Bruce.

The purpose of this research is to examine the impact of the policy on sentencer decision making by providing results which will enable:

- an assessment of the impact of arrangements for the implementation of the National Standards on sentencers' use of non-custodial disposals;

- an assessment of the relationship between sentencers' perceptions of decision making and local practice;

- an assessment of the impact of local liaison arrangements on shrieval decision making.

THE IMPACT OF THE POLICY ON THE USE OF CUSTODY

The judiciary are bound by legislation, not social work criminal justice policy. However, the policy is intended to improve the quality and availability of community based court disposals and the quality of Social Enquiry Reports (SERs) which assist sentencer decision making. The policy can therefore have an indirect impact on sentencing decisions.

The analysis of Scottish Office criminal justice statistics identified a slight increase in the use of custody since the introduction of the policy in 1991, which is contrary to the expectations of the policy. A reduction in the use of short custodial sentences and a slight increase in the use of probation for younger offenders since 1991 were identified and are consistent with policy objectives. However, there are many factors which can influence sentencing trends, such as an increase in the incidence of more serious offences, and thus it is difficult to isolate the impact of the policy from other factors.

The findings of this study have identified a range of factors which can influence sentencers' decisions to impose a custodial rather than a community based disposal: characteristics of the offence; characteristics of the offender; the quality of SERs; the availability of services; and the credibility of community based disposals. However, the fundamental concern which sheriffs expressed was in relation to the public interest and safety which often led to a focus on risk of re-offending.

Characteristics of the Offence

Sheriffs indicated that the gravity of the offence was a main consideration in borderline cases. They said that they would tend to impose a custodial sentence for serious offences where there was a need to protect the public, community service for serious offences where that need was absent and probation for less serious offences (and where the SER identified a problem which could be addressed through probation and the offender was willing to cooperate).

In some areas sheriffs indicated that they would impose a custodial sentence as a deterrent for certain types of offence whose incidence had increased. However, at the individual level, social workers thought that probation might be more successful in reducing the risk of re-offending in some of these cases.

Characteristics of the Offender

Factors relating to the offender which influenced sheriffs' decisions included: the risk of their re-offending; their motivation to stop offending; the existence of a problem which could be addressed through probation; their willingness to cooperate; whether they were repeat offenders; and their previous experience of a community based disposal. Sheriffs stated that they tended to use custody for repeat offenders as a last resort after community based disposals had been considered or previously tried.

Sheriffs reported that they looked to the SER to provide information and assessments about the offender and that these influenced their decision. Thus it is important that SERs provide sentencers with the information which they require.

Quality of SERs

Although sheriffs were generally satisfied with the quality of reports, the reports in the study sample did not always provide the key information which sheriffs sought (such as the pattern of offending and risk of re-offending), nor did they fully meet the more extensive requirements of the National Standards. The reasons provided by social workers for certain information not being presented included: the information may have been obtained but was not deemed relevant; pressure of work and administrative delays; delays in accessing other agencies; problems in accessing a full list of previous convictions; and problems in obtaining full details of the offence. The latter hindered the social worker's assessment of the offender's attitude to the offence and thus the offender's level of commitment as a potential probationer. Social workers reported that if they had to rely on the offender's version alone, there was a danger that their assessment for a community based disposal could become inappropriate and viewed by sheriffs as unrealistic. In such cases, their recommendation would be unlikely to be followed.

Although court social workers and social work managers acknowledged that there had been an improvement in the quality of SERs since the introduction of the National Standards, they recognised that there was scope for further improvements, for example, by authors taking a more analytic approach rather than being descriptive. It was found that social work departments in the study areas were committed to monitoring and improving the quality of SERs.

Sixty-five per cent of the SER recommendations in the study sample were followed. There was no difference in the level of "missing" information (in respect of the requirements of the National Standards) between reports where the recommendation was accepted or rejected. Most sheriffs said that they would tend to follow a recommendation if it was realistic, was based on the body of the report and took into account the gravity of the offence. However, as social workers had difficulty in accessing full details of the offence, assessments of the gravity of the offence and the presentation of a realistic recommendation were problematic.

Availability of Services

One of the policy objectives was to increase the quantity of specialist services and some were established in the study areas shortly after the policy was introduced in 1991. Despite this, social workers in each area and some sheriffs identified gaps in the range and quantity of provision of specialist services which, sheriffs said, could influence their use of custody. The number of places available on specialist initiatives was relatively small compared to the total number of persons convicted in each court.

Credibility of Community based Court Disposals

Most sheriffs reported that community service continued to be viewed as a credible disposal and that probation had achieved greater credibility since the introduction of the policy. Although Scottish Office statistics demonstrated a slight increase in the use of probation since 1991, the study of probation in this programme found that probation supervision in the study areas had not fully met the National Standards by summer 1995.

Some sheriffs indicated that they would welcome more detailed feedback on the success of orders imposed on "high risk" offenders than that supplied by completion reports. (Some sheriffs said that they might prefer to impose a deferred sentence than probation for "high risk" cases as they were then able to retain control over the offender by requesting bi-monthly reports.)

Feedback to sentencers on the success of community based court disposals is an important factor in increasing the credibility of these disposals for "high risk" offenders. This can be achieved by providing sentencers with more detailed completion reports on individual "high risk" cases and by providing detailed local and national assessments of the success of community based disposals for "high risk" cases. The main forum for providing information on success of community based disposals is formal liaison meetings between the local social work department and the judiciary.

THE IMPACT OF THE POLICY ON LIAISON

Informal liaison with court social workers, designed to deal with day-to-day problems as they arise, was said by both sheriffs and court social workers to be operating well and to have improved as a result of the appointment of specific court social workers. The National Standards also encourage the establishment of formal liaison meetings between sheriffs and the social work department to discuss strategic issues such as the amount and range of service provision and the information required by sentencers about the outcome of disposals. However, it was found that formal liaison meetings where such issues were discussed tended not to take place in the study areas. It was suggested that feedback of information to sentencers is required to reduce the uncertainty about the effectiveness of new penal policies before changes in sentencing outcomes become apparent.

However, the study on the national and local context within this programme found that social work departments may not, at the time of the research, have been in a position to provide information on the success of community based disposals, as local and national management information systems had not been fully operational.

CONCLUSION

It is evident that, by the end of the research fieldwork (summer 1995), the policy had not been fully implemented in relation to: the availability and quality of community based services; the quality of SERs; effective formal liaison arrangements; and the feedback of information on the success of community based disposals. It is thus perhaps not surprising that the policy objective of reducing the use of custody had not been achieved by the end of 1994. However, it is acknowledged that sentencing trends can be influenced by factors other than policy implementation.

It is encouraging to note that, although the research covered the early stages of policy implementation and that further improvements could be made, significant progress had been achieved and there was some indication that the use of probation in the study areas had increased.

CHAPTER ONE
BACKGROUND TO THE STUDY

INTRODUCTION

In Scotland, statutory social work services to offenders and their families are provided by the local authority social work departments. Since April 1991, the Scottish Office has reimbursed to social work departments the full costs of providing a range of statutory social work services in the criminal justice system. National Objectives and Standards (the National Standards) were introduced by the Social Work Services Group of the Scottish Office to coincide with the introduction of the funding initiative. The aim of the National Standards is to promote the development of high quality management and practice, the most efficient and effective use of resources and to provide social work services to the criminal justice system which have the confidence of both the courts and the wider public.

The National Standards and the funding initiative cover: social enquiry reports; court social work services; probation; community service[1]; and throughcare (social work in prisons is funded by the Scottish Prison Service). Since 1991, the initiative has been extended to supervised release orders, bail information and accommodation schemes, and supervised attendance order schemes (the latter two schemes are not yet available on a national basis). It is intended to include diversion from prosecution in the 100 per cent funding arrangement, subject to the progress of pilot schemes to be established in 1996. At present, fine supervision, means enquiry reports and deferred sentence supervision are not included in the funding initiative.

Prior to the introduction of the 100 per cent funding initiative and the National Standards, local authorities had to fund the majority of social work services out of their general income. Criminal justice services were, therefore, in competition for resources with other local authority services and as a result were not always of sufficient quantity and quality to meet the requirements of the courts.

The main aims of the Government's policy are[2]:

- to reduce the use of custody by increasing the availability, improving the quality and targeting the use of community based court disposals and throughcare services on those most at risk of custody, especially young adult repeat offenders;

- to enable offenders to address their offending behaviour and make a successful adjustment to law abiding life.

BACKGROUND TO THE RESEARCH

Central Government's review and evaluation of implementation of the funding initiative and the National Standards involves a programme of inspection by Social Work Services Inspectorate (SWSI), interpretation of statistics and a programme of research.

The research programme is being conducted in three phases. The main purpose of Phase One, which was undertaken in 1993, was to examine the responses of key criminal justice decision makers and Scottish Office officials to the principal objectives of the policy and the early arrangements for its implementation (McAra, 1998). Phase Two (of which this study is a part) consists of five inter-related studies, conducted in 1994-1995, which examine progress towards policy objectives: the national and local context of policy implementation (Brown, Levy and McIvor, 1998); sentencer decision making (Brown and Levy, 1998); Parole Board decision making (McAra, 1998a); the process and outcomes of probation (McIvor and Barry, 1998); and the process and outcomes of throughcare (McIvor and Barry, 1998a). Phase Three will look at the longer term impact of services for offenders.

Four sheriff court areas, each in separate social work authorities, were selected as study sites for the research programme to reflect areas of both high and low population density and to represent both specialist and more generic forms of organising social work criminal justice services. The names of the four areas have been anonymised in reports and are referred to as Scott, Wallace, Burns and Bruce.

---

[1] The 100% funding initiative and National Objectives and Standards were first applied to community service in 1989.

[2] Evaluation Strategy Working Group, September 1990. More recent statements (the 1996 White Paper on Crime and Punishment, paragraphs 9.1 and 10.3) are consistent with these aims.

In order to achieve the principal objectives it was recognised that a number of intermediate objectives would need to be achieved and these have been evaluated by the research programme:

1. To improve and strengthen the quality and credibility of community based disposals available to the courts by setting out and securing the implementation of clearly stated standards and priorities.

2. To increase the credibility of community based disposals available to the court by ensuring that National Standards are met.

3. To ensure that the needs of the court are met in terms of an adequate supply of community based disposals of the required quality.

4. To ensure liaison arrangements exist between the social work departments and the courts which are capable of meeting the court's needs for social work services.

5. To ensure the development of services specifically aimed as those at increased risk of custody, in particular young adult offenders and their needs.

6. To improve the quality of statutory and non-statutory supervision of released prisoners so as to encourage earlier release on licence and compliance with licence requirements. To improve the service provided by social work departments to released prisoners not subject to statutory supervision.

7. To ensure that organisation and management are such as to deliver the services effectively and efficiently.

8. To ensure that the provision and the use of services are monitored to establish the extent to which the initiative's objectives are being met.

(Evaluation Strategy Working Group, 1990)

The purpose of this study is to examine the impact of the policy on sentencer decision making.

Methods

In order to determine whether there had been any change in the use of custody since the introduction of the policy in April 1991, sentencing patterns in each of the sample courts and for sheriff courts in Scotland as a whole were identified. These were based on an analysis of The Scottish Office criminal justice statistics 1989 to 1994.

An analysis of a sample of social enquiry reports (SERs) was used to identify issues to be raised in interviews and to explore the relationship between social work recommendations and disposals. A quota sample was requested from each study site of the most recent reports recommending: probation (20); community service (20); deferred sentence with some form of social work (10); and reports which made no recommendation (10) or where the author was unable to offer a recommendation. It should be noted that as this was a quota sample (in which a predetermined number of each type of recommendation was selected), the results of the analyses cannot be interpreted as being representative of all of the SERs prepared in each court. The sample was selected to provide a basis from which to explore the features of different types of recommendation. The reports provided by each area are shown in Table 1.1.

Table 1.1: Recommendations of Reports in the SER Sample

Recommendation	Scott	Wallace	Burns	Bruce
Probation	20	19	20	20
Community Service	20	19	20	20
Deferred Sentence	7	*	2	5
No recommendation	10	10	10	10
Total	57	48	52	55

*Wallace did not offer courts the opportunity to impose deferred sentence with social work support

Interviews were conducted in spring 1995 with seven sheriffs resident in the courts from which the SER sample was selected. Their views were sought regarding the role of the SER, the credibility of community based disposals, liaison arrangements and other factors which influenced their sentencing decisions. A representative from the procurator fiscal's office for each court was interviewed (except one where the researcher was unable to arrange an appointment) to obtain their views on breach procedures, diversion and liaison arrangements. A court social worker and a group of four social workers from each study area were interviewed regarding the quality and preparation of SERs and liaison arrangements.

Where relevant, results of other studies in the research programme are included. A more detailed discussion of the methods is presented in Annex II.

Structure of The Report

Chapter Two sets the context of the study by examining the social work services provided to the court and the organisational structures of each study area. The views of sentencers and social workers on the credibility, quality and availability of these services are provided and are linked later in the report to assessments of sentencing trends.

The factors which influence sentencer decision making are explored in Chapter Three and an assessment is made of the extent to which social work services can impact on sentencing decisions. Chapter Four compares the information which sheriffs and social workers identified as key information to be provided in SERs with the guidance provided in the National Standards and the information provided by the reports in the SER sample. The significance of differences between the information provided and perceptions of the quality of SERs is explored.

Chapter Five relates to sentencing decisions. Firstly, sentencing trends in the study courts and all sheriff courts in Scotland are examined to assess whether the policy objective of reducing the use of custody has been achieved. Secondly, the extent to which SER recommendations coincide with the disposal imposed, and possible reasons for discrepancies, are explored.

The final chapter assesses the extent to which the policy has impacted on social work practice and sentencing decisions. Factors which have inhibited and those which have facilitated the impact of the policy on sentencing decisions are explored.

CHAPTER TWO

SOCIAL WORK SERVICES AND ORGANISATIONAL STRUCTURES

INTRODUCTION

The purpose of this chapter is to provide the context for the later discussion on factors which influence sentencer decision making. The objectives of social work services to the court are described, summarising the guidance provided in the National Standards. The changes in organisational structures which have taken place as a result of policy implementation and the specialist services available in each of the study areas are then described. Finally, sentencers' views on the credibility and availability of community disposals are presented to provide an indication of the impact of these aspects of social work services on sentencing decisions.

SUMMARY OF THE OBJECTIVES AND STANDARDS OF SOCIAL WORK SERVICES TO THE COURT[3]

The Role of the Social Enquiry Reports

Social enquiry reports (SERs) and associated court services form part of a wider range of services. These services are intended to increase and promote opportunities for courts and prosecutors to reduce the use of custody and prosecution to the minimum required in the public interest and to promote social welfare. SERs are prepared for the courts by local authority social work departments. The relevant criminal justice legislation requires the court to obtain a report before making a probation order[4] or a community service order[5] and before imposing either a first sentence of imprisonment on any offender aged 21 or over, or any sentence of detention on an offender between the ages of 16 and 20. Imprisonment or detention may only be imposed if the court is of the opinion that no other method of dealing with the offender is appropriate[6]. (National Standards 1991, part two (SERs), paragraphs 1 and 2.)

SERs are intended as an aid to sentencing. They provide the court with reliable information and analysis on those aspects of offenders' circumstances and personality which have a bearing on their offending behaviour; they may comment on the suitability of offenders for specific community based disposals; and, where certain categories of offenders are at risk of a custodial sentence, they must assist the court's consideration of whether other disposals are feasible. An important aspect of the preparation of an SER is its focus on offending behaviour and it should provide information relevant to the understanding of offending behaviour. The author of the SER should be prepared to comment on subjects' perceptions of their culpability, the seriousness of their offending behaviour and its impact on their victim. The SER should never be a plea in mitigation. (National Standards 1991, part 2 (SERs) paragraphs 3 and 4.)

Other Court Services

Social workers are sometimes requested to provide other reports to the court. Oral[7] and stand down reports[8] provide specific information which may make it possible for the court to deal with a case without requesting an SER or to continue a case on bail rather than to remand in custody or to suggest that an SER or other report might be helpful. Pre-trial reports are requested for certain cases where people charged under solemn procedure plead not guilty. Court social workers represent the social work department in the court setting and liaise with other professional groups. They provide a range of services to the court including dealing with requests for reports and monitoring their standards; and interviewing offenders following a request for a report, a custodial sentence or remand, or a disposal involving social work services. Court social workers also provide other services including the provision of information and advice to the families and friends of offenders and accused people and to witnesses and victims of crime. (National Standards 1991, part 2 (SERs), paragraphs 1, 99 to 111.)

---

[3] The National Standards 1991.

[4] Criminal Justice (Scotland) Act 1987.

[5] Community Service by Offenders (Scotland) Act 1978. (Most legislation regarding social enquiry reports is now consolidated into the Criminal Procedure (Scotland) Act 1995.)

[6] Criminal Procedure (Scotland) Act 1975 as amended by sections 42 and 45 of the Criminal Justice (Scotland) Act 1980.

[7] A social worker may make an oral report to the court where he/she has not had the time necessary to provide a written report.

[8] The court may sometimes request an immediate oral or written report from a court social worker during the course of court proceedings and adjourn the case until later in the day for this to be done.

Probation Orders

The National Standards state that probation orders are intended to serve the following main objectives:

(a) To serve as a credible community based disposal which requires the offender to work towards an acknowledgement of responsibility for offending behaviour and seeks to reduce the risk of reoffending by combining supervision and control with help, encouragement and challenge.

(b) To extend the community based options available to the court where the current and previous pattern of offending would have placed offenders either at immediate risk of custody or likely to be at such risk in the foreseeable future.

(National Standards 1991, part 2 (Probation), paragraph 7.)

Probation combines elements of control and assistance and should therefore normally only be recommended where there is a need for both. There should also be evidence that the offender can be motivated to use probation supervision to help them to address problems and issues associated with his/her offending behaviour. Greatest priority should be afforded those offenders at risk of custody who have significant underlying problems and who are likely to re-offend or who are repeat offenders. (National Standards 1991, part 2 (Probation), paragraphs 11 to 13.)

Probation orders can have additional requirements attached, for example, to attend for psychiatric treatment, to undertake community service (section 7 orders) or to attend an intensive probation programme (IPP). Section 7 orders should only be used when, in view of the seriousness of the offence and the personal circumstances of the offender, neither a probation order nor a section 1 community service order is considered appropriate. IPPs are demanding in time, involve systematic and rigorous supervision, and place heavy commitments and strict standards of behaviour on the offender. When recommending an IPP, SER writers should satisfy themselves that: the offender is at serious risk of a custodial sentence; other disposals including probation and section 7 probation orders have been tried and/or are not considered appropriate; and the offender has been assessed as suitable for the project. (National Standards 1991, part 2 (Probation), paragraphs 35 to 43.)

Community Service Orders

Community service was made available to all criminal courts in Scotland from 1978 and National Standards were introduced in 1989. Detailed information on community service is provided in the Standards. The main objectives for community service by offenders include the following:

(a) to provide criminal courts with a credible community based penalty, by requiring those found guilty of imprisonable offences and who would otherwise have received a custodial sentence, to undertake unpaid work for a specified number of hours for the community;

(b) to seek to ensure that community service is only recommended and used where other community based disposals for dealing with the offender are not appropriate.

(National Standards 1991, part 2 (Probation), paragraph 1.)

Community service should present a challenge to the offender. The punitive element in the penalty is contained in the time which offenders must devote to community service work, in the essential disciplines of regular attendance, prompt timekeeping, and satisfactory work performance, and in the prompt application of disciplinary procedures for non-compliance. (National Standards 1991, part 2 (Probation), paragraph 10.)

Deferred Sentence with Social Work Services

The main differences between a deferred sentence with social work services and probation are that the deferred sentence does not provide for regular supervision of the offender except on a voluntary basis and has little means of enforcing compliance with conditions attached to it. The offender is subject to sentence at the end of the period of deferment.

This social work service is not 100 per cent funded and, at the time of the research, was only provided to courts with the agreement of the social work department. In one of the study areas (Wallace), the social work department had not agreed to provide this service as sufficient resources were not available.

Other Social Work Criminal Justice Services

Although this study focuses on decisions about and recommendations for probation, community service and deferred sentence, there are two other relevant social work criminal justice services: diversion and supervised attendance orders. Diversion from prosecution is a service in which social work departments offer a service to procurators fiscal to enable them to divert certain alleged offenders from prosecution by providing a social work service as an alternative. Supervised attendance orders can be imposed on fine defaulters as an alternative to custody, involving a period of constructive activity in the community. The court disposals which do not involve social work services but should be addressed in the SER are the fine, compensation orders and admonition.

ORGANISATIONAL STRUCTURES

The National Standards

One of the general principles of the National Standards is that social work services to the criminal justice system must be organised in such a way that the courts would have confidence in their availability and effectiveness. Although the National Standards expected criminal justice social work services to be provided by specialist staff devoted full-time to such work, especially in urban areas, it was acknowledged that a more flexible approach would be required in smaller rural areas. (National Standards 1991, part I, paragraphs 13 and 29).

The National Standards acknowledged the variety of organisational structures which had existed previously and indicated that it was the responsibility of each local authority to decide on the detailed service arrangements necessary in their area, although they were required to consult with SWSG about the organisational and management systems they proposed to adopt. (National Standards 1991, part I, paragraph 28). As a result, a range of organisational structures was established throughout Scotland.

Organisational Structures of the Study Areas

The study areas were selected partly on the basis of their differing organisational structures to enable the evaluation to take account of the range of contexts within which the policy must be operated. The changes in the organisational structures of the four study areas are outlined in Table 2.1.

Table 2.1: Changes in Organisational Structures

	Scott	Wallace	Burns	Bruce
Pre-1991 Structure	Generic teams but some social workers specialised in CJ work.	Specialist teams since 1990.	Generic teams.	Generic teams but some social workers specialised in CJ work.
New Structure	Specialist workers up to 80 per cent of whose time is allocated to CJ work. Generic middle management. (1991)	Specialist up to senior management level (1990).	Specialist to middle management level (1991).	Specialist teams with generic middle management (1992).
Court Services Pre-1991	One full-time court social worker and two specialist social workers attached to teams on a rota basis.	Specialist social workers on a rota basis.	One part-time specialist social worker attached to a generic team.	Specialist social workers on a rota basis.
New Court Services	Two full-time court social workers plus two administrative staff.	Two full-time court social workers with small caseload.	Two part-time court social workers.	Three part-time specialist social workers.

STAFFORDSHIRE UNIVERSITY LIBRARY

The organisational arrangements for community service varied in the four areas. In Scott, community service teams were structurally separate from other areas of criminal justice social work services. In Bruce and Wallace, steps had been taken to integrate community service in offender teams, whereas in Burns progress towards integration was slow.

The organisational changes undertaken as a result of policy implementation were radical in most areas and it is likely that these changes would require some time to settle before an improved quality of services could be achieved. The Standards were partially based on examples of good practice and thus the approach to service delivery by some areas may have been consistent with that advocated by certain sections of the Standards prior to their introduction. As the study areas were at different stages in policy implementation it would be expected that the impact of the policy would be at variable stages. For example, in Wallace, the shift to specialisation took place in 1990 whereas in Bruce reorganisation did not take place until October 1992, one year after Scott and Burns.

The specialist projects for offenders on statutory orders available at the time of the research in the four study areas are listed in Table 2.2.

Table 2.2: Specialist Projects for Offenders in the Study Areas

	Scott	Wallace	Burns	Bruce
Intensive Probation	SWD (1988)	Independent (1991)	Independent (1991)	Informal
Substance Misuse	SWD (1991)	Independent (pre-1991)	SWD (1995)	Independent (1992)
Alcohol Misuse	Independent (1990)	Independent (pre-1991)	Independent (1991)	Independent (1990)
Mental Health	Independent (1992)	SWD (1993)	None	None
Sex Offenders	None	SWD (1990)	None	None
Domestic Violence	None	None	Independent (1991)	None
Employment	None	Independent (1990)	Independent (1991)	Independent (1992)
Supported Accommodation	None	Independent (1990-94)	Independent (1992)	None

Local authority plans[9] examined as part of the study on the national and local context (Brown, Levy and McIvor, 1998), showed that in the early stages of implementation most authorities tended to focus on organisational changes and on enhancing and developing existing services rather than introducing substantial new initiatives. However, although plans contained proposals for new initiatives, subsequent plans reported that sufficient funding was not available to implement many of these proposed developments. Reviews of service delivery in local authority plans indicated that the National Standards were unlikely to be fully implemented by 1993/94. The extent to which this might have impacted on sentencers' views of the credibility of services was explored in order to determine whether this might have influenced their use of these services.

---

[9] Scott: Annual Planning Statements, 1993-95. Strategic Plans, 1992-94.
Wallace: Planning Statement, 1992-93. Regional Management and Budget Reports, 1991-92.
Strategic Plans, 1994-97.
Burns: Annual Planning Statements, 1993-97. Strategic Plans, 1992-94.
Bruce: Annual Planning Statements, 1993-97. Strategic Plans, 1992-96.

THE CREDIBILITY AND AVAILABILITY OF SERVICES

Phase One (McAra, 1998) identified three factors which increased judicial confidence in a disposal: feedback on the process and outcome of supervision; a well written SER; and guaranteed funding for services. Findings of this study were consistent with those in Phase One.

Views about the credibility and availability of community disposals were sought from sheriffs, social work managers,[10] court social workers and team social workers in the study authorities. It was found that, overall, sheriffs generally considered services to be credible. However, some sheriffs, court social workers and social workers considered that there was a need for some additional specialist services in their local area. Their views were obtained in respect of probation and community service.

Credibility of Probation

Sheriffs stated that the quality of probation had improved as a result of the implementation of the National Standards. For example, they suggested that probation had increased in credibility since the introduction of the National Standards, partly because of the improvements in social enquiry reports and assessments, but mainly because probation was better structured, and they were more confident that supervision would be undertaken. Both sheriffs and social workers reported that, prior to the National Standards, probationers in some areas might never have been or have been rarely seen during their order. Sheriffs indicated that they had more confidence in using probation as an alternative to custody since the National Standards, as reports now put forward proposals on problems to be tackled through probation within an action plan.

Interviews with sheriffs conducted in 1993 as part of Phase One of the research programme (McAra, 1998) indicated that sheriffs at that time were satisfied with probation services. Some of these sheriffs identified substantial improvements as a direct result of implementation of the Standards, such as improved levels of supervision and as a result of receiving regular feedback on the progress and outcome of the order. Other sheriffs had noted a more gradual improvement in probation services, mainly attributed to the shift to greater specialisation amongst some social workers.

In this study, sheriffs generally had difficulty in identifying the need for any changes to their local probation service, because they were satisfied with the present service or, for some sheriffs, because they did not know what happened in a probation order as completion reports did not give any details. Ford, Ditton and Laybourn (1992)[11] found that sheriffs' lack of confidence in probation supervision was a result of a lack of knowledge about the process and lack of feedback (also delays in allocation and not breaching when faced with difficulties).

Concerns were expressed by some sheriffs in our study which they thought might be related to resources, for example, the length of time taken to implement the order, and the frequency of contact with probationers. Despite this, it would appear that there was consensus amongst most sheriffs that probation was operated as a rigorous programme. The National Standards were seen as setting out a good framework for probation and, provided that Standards were adhered to, sheriffs indicated that they would have confidence in probation.

Social work managers (Brown, Levy and McIvor, 1998) and social workers also thought that the National Standards and training had brought about significant improvements in probation practice. The areas in which the greatest progress was said by managers to have been made in introducing more structured offence focused methods of work were those which had the clearest specialist structures. McIvor and Barry (1998) found that the area in which social workers' time was not fully allocated to criminal justice work (Scott), tended to adopt the more traditional approach of one-to-one work to address offending behaviour. The researchers suggested that it was possible that the additional pressures created by split posts, through conflicting demands on staff time, may have prevented the introduction of more innovative methods of work. Despite this, McIvor and Barry found that National Standards were being more consistently met in that area and that staff appeared to be clearly operating within the model of probation practice advocated by the Standards.

Social work managers considered that the Standards had introduced greater clarity about the procedures to be adopted with non-compliance and in the evidential requirements for breach. This view was confirmed by procurators fiscal. McIvor and Barry found that the differing levels of breach amongst the study areas were more closely related to the types of offender in the probation samples than the different organisational structures: the area with the highest tariff offenders (Wallace) had the highest breach rates.

---

[10] Interviews with 12 middle and senior social work managers in the four study authorities were obtained as part of the study on the national and local context (Brown, Levy and McIvor, 1998).

[11] Ford, R., Ditton, J. and Laybourn, A. (1992). *Probation in Scotland: Access and Practice.* The Scottish Office Central Research Unit.

Credibility of Community Service

Most sheriffs also held positive views about the credibility of community service and thought that the schemes were operated efficiently. They considered that community service obliged the offender to respond positively and not simply be passive and that offenders benefited from the discipline imposed by introducing them to the concept of work and giving them self-respect. This was seen as particularly relevant to young offenders who might not have worked before. Community service was also viewed as being of benefit to the community. One sheriff considered that the community service and supervised attendance order schemes had been reasonably successful in moving people on into employment and training. Only one sheriff (Burns) said that sometimes he could not impose community service when he would like to because the scheme was full.

Social workers thought that sheriffs regarded community service as a credible disposal as social workers were now much stricter about warnings and obtaining reasons for non-attendance or lateness. Social work managers generally agreed that the new funding arrangements had had less impact upon the quality of community service practice since it had always been a relatively "tight ship". However, not all areas had fully integrated community service within offender services teams at the time of the research.

Availability of Services

Sheriffs considered that the increase in availability of specialist services had been helpful. Despite a slight increase in the range of available services since the introduction of the policy (Table 2.2), the social workers (and a few sheriffs) identified a need for further services which could be provided as a condition of a probation order or on a voluntary basis during a period of deferred sentence. (As noted earlier, local authorities identified in their plans a need for further services but had difficulty in obtaining funding for these services.)

Intensive Probation

The introduction of intensive probation was welcomed by many sheriffs who had confidence in using this as an alternative to custody and they acknowledged that it was not an "easy option". However, in Bruce, the more rural area, an appropriate intensive probation course might not always be available due to the resources and demand at any one time. In interviews with sheriffs, a view was expressed that a lack of appropriate places might discourage sheriffs from imposing a probation order.

Substance Misuse Services

Social workers from Burns, Bruce and Scott reported that there were insufficient local substance misuse services to meet demand. In Scott, places on the drugs misuse project occasionally became available too late in an order, or in some cases after the order had been completed. Social workers were therefore sometimes reluctant to recommend a probation order with a condition of substance misuse counselling.

Supervised and Supported Accommodation

In each of the four study areas, social workers reported a lack of supported accommodation for people who might receive probation or community service orders or those who could be granted bail. In Burns a voluntary organisation provided a service for younger offenders but there was no accommodation service for the homeless older offender and sometimes sheriffs placed them on remand as there was no alternative accommodation for these people. In Scott and Bruce, social workers were reluctant to refer some offenders for residential and other services outwith their local areas to urban centres as it was believed that they could be exposed to further risk or find it difficult to cope in a strange environment.

Some sheriffs identified a lack of a residential hostel as an impediment to imposing community service or probation on those offenders with an unstable living arrangement which, in some instances, may have resulted in them giving a custodial sentence. A stable residential situation was seen to be essential to allow community service work to be carried out and to enable ready communication with the supervising officer.

Services for Violent Offenders

In Wallace, social workers identified a need for specialist probation projects targeting particular groups of offenders such as violent offenders. The intensive probation project and the project for domestic violence in Burns were only available for those on a statutory order and social workers would have liked to have seen these services having been made available to offenders on a voluntary basis.

Mental Health Services

Social workers in Burns also identified a need for further services for people with mental health problems as they considered the medical agencies to be unwilling or unable to provide a service to offenders. In Scott, social workers considered that mental health services were insufficient to meet demand. One sheriff in Bruce identified a need for local mental health services as he considered that the value of probation would be lessened if the offender had to travel long distances for treatment to "an otherwise inhospitable and alien environment".

Services in Rural Areas

Social workers in Bruce acknowledged that demand for the more specialist services could be erratic in rural areas and could thus be difficult to finance and organise. Social work managers considered that the relatively low numbers requiring specialist services in rural areas precluded the development of locally based initiatives and served as a disincentive to organisations providing services in more densely populated areas to extend these services on an outreach basis to outlying areas. However, one independent sector provider provided an employment service on an outreach basis to offenders in Bruce.

Services for Young Offenders

The National Standards were considered by Phase One interviewees (McAra, 1998) to have had minimal impact on the development of specialist services. Intensive probation was targeted on young people committing more serious offences. Concerns were expressed that insufficient attention had been given to the development of schemes aimed at young people involved in less serious offences.

Although the level of available funding influences the level of service provision, it is important that service planners receive views from sentencers and practitioners about the need for specialist services. Liaison meetings between sentencers and the social work department provide a forum where such needs can be discussed.

LIAISON ARRANGEMENTS

The National Standards emphasise the importance of developing good liaison arrangements with sentencers and other agencies to ensure that the new arrangements work well. Such liaison was seen to be necessary both at the informal level to deal with problems as they arose and at the formal level to discuss strategic issues including: the range, quality and quantity of service provision; priorities; and the information required by sentencers about the outcome of disposals.

The formal and informal liaison arrangements in existence in the four study areas at the time of the research are illustrated in Table 2.3.

Table 2.3: Liaison Arrangements

	Formal	Informal
Scott	Court social worker attends the Court Consultative Committee.	Ad hoc liaison between court social workers and sheriffs, and between social workers and procurators fiscal.
Wallace	Sheriffs attend formal liaison meetings with senior social work managers.	Ad hoc liaison between court social workers and sheriffs and between social workers and procurators fiscal.
Burns	Sheriffs attend formal liaison meetings with senior social work managers. Team managers attend court users' meetings.	Ad hoc liaison between court social workers and sheriffs and between social workers and procurators fiscal.
Bruce	Sheriff attends local team's annual review meeting.	Ad hoc liaison between sheriffs and court social workers and district manager. Ad hoc liaison between social workers and procurator fiscal.

Where sheriffs attended formal liaison meetings they sometimes viewed these as a waste of time seeing them primarily as a "window-dressing" opportunity for the social work department. Although the Burns sheriffs were consulted about their views on social work services, when there was a complaint, for example, about SERs not being submitted in time, the problem was not always resolved. Other sheriffs indicated that they were not consulted about new initiatives before they were developed and did not consider this to be appropriate (but were informed about them prior to their implementation). However, some of these sheriffs indicated that they would have welcomed feedback on how well offenders, particularly "high risk" offenders, had performed their community service or probation orders, as completion reports did not provide this information. Formal liaison meetings would have provided a forum for such feedback.

Sheriffs indicated that they preferred dealing with the social work department on an informal and more practical level, such as contacting the court social workers or team manager on an ad hoc basis, an arrangement which they found to be adequate and in which problems could be discussed and resolved.

In one area the court social workers said that they would like to have had more meetings with sheriffs but sheriffs had declined and had declined invitations to other meetings, for example, with the offender services team. In another area, social workers had expressed a desire to attend liaison meetings with sheriffs as they considered that the issues discussed were relevant to their work.

Although, in general, the sheriffs could not identify any changes made in liaison arrangements since the Standards and did not identify a need for change, they stressed the importance of stability of staff which allowed relationships and trust to develop, both in relation to court social workers and other court staff. As one sheriff said: "A lot of the system depends on trust and knowing which people you can rely on".

Factors which Facilitate Liaison:

- Where social workers had previously covered the court on a rota basis, it was difficult for them to build up relationships with sentencers. Since specific court social workers were appointed, they considered that informal liaison had improved. In some areas, especially in a smaller court, relationships with the court were reported by sheriffs to be good because everyone knew each other and "things get organised".

- The senior court social worker in Scott reported that she held a training event at the time of the introduction of the Standards for sheriffs to meet with the heads of various projects providing a service as a condition of a probation order and the community service project leader. She reported that a sheriff who was reluctant to use community service, subsequently held more positive views about that disposal.

Factors which Inhibit Liaison:

- In Wallace, court social workers did not have an office in the court which may have hindered sheriffs, other court staff, offenders and their families from contacting them. A court social worker from that area reported that they did not have much contact with sheriffs but they were "very approachable".

- The large number of visiting or temporary sheriffs in certain courts seemed to inhibit effective liaison as they did not visit one court on a regular basis.

CONCLUSION

Sheriffs, social work managers and social workers considered that some progress had been made towards achieving policy objectives.

The quality and credibility of probation was considered to have improved significantly since the introduction of the policy, whereas community service was viewed as credible prior to the 1991 policy. (National Standards for community service were introduced in 1989.) However, it was found that only a limited success had been achieved in increasing the range of specialist services. Most specialist services had been introduced in the study areas prior to, or shortly after, the introduction of the policy but few additional services had been established since then. Gaps in service provision were identified by social workers and some sheriffs. These sheriffs suggested that the lack of appropriate specialist services, such as supported accommodation, could inhibit their use of community based disposals.

The policy objective of ensuring the existence of liaison arrangements which meet the court's needs was partly achieved. Informal liaison was said by sheriffs and social workers to have operated well. However, some sheriffs identified a need for more detailed feedback on the outcome of community based disposals for "high risk" offenders. Formal liaison meetings should provide an opportunity for such feedback, in addition to other strategic issues, but some sheriffs were reluctant to attend formal meetings.

CHAPTER THREE
FACTORS WHICH INFLUENCE SENTENCER DECISION MAKING

INTRODUCTION

This chapter examines the factors which influence sentencer decision making by exploring the circumstances in which sentencers would impose a community based disposal as opposed to a custodial sentence. These are compared with factors which influence social workers' recommendations for disposal in the SER. An assessment is then made of the extent to which social work services can impact on sentencer decision making.

FACTORS WHICH INFLUENCE SENTENCERS' DECISIONS

Sheriffs were asked to identify the factors which influenced their use of custody and the factors which might influence their decision to use a community based disposal in borderline cases, distinguishing between community service and probation. The fundamental concern which sheriffs expressed was in relation to the public interest and safety which often led to a focus on risk of re-offending in individual cases. Sheriffs stressed that they did not target groups of offenders such as young offenders or types of offence when considering the disposal but looked at each individual case, as the most appropriate disposal depended on the circumstances of the case. Despite their reluctance to make broad generalisations, sheriffs did identify some factors which might influence their sentencing decisions. These can be grouped into three categories: factors relating to the offence; the offender; and social work services.

Factors relating to the offence included the type and gravity of offence. In some areas, sheriffs reported that the incidence of offences such as the carrying of knives, housebreaking and theft of a motor vehicle had increased and that the police had mounted a campaign against such offences. Sheriffs indicated that these offences might thus attract a custodial sentence as a deterrent. Gravity of the offence was also viewed by sheriffs as a major factor in their sentencing decision.

Sheriffs mentioned factors relating to the offender such as the existence of a problem which could be addressed through probation, the willingness of the offender to cooperate, their motivation to stop offending and whether they were repeat offenders. They also referred to factors relating to social work services, such as previous experience of a community-based disposal and the availability of specialist services.

The main factors which influenced decisions about whether to impose a custodial or community based disposal are presented in Table 3.1.

Table 3.1: Factors Influencing Sentencing Decisions

Disposal	Factors Influencing Decision
Custody	Gravity of offence - where it is considered to indicate that custody is in the public interest, or that it will protect the public As a last resort When there has been disregard for an order of the court If there is a high incidence of a particular type of offence within the locality Where an offender lacks a stable residence and there is no supported accommodation available
Community Service	For serious offences where offender's problems have not been, or are not capable of being resolved through probation Where an offender could benefit from disciplined work offering reparation to community
Probation	Where an SER has identified a problem which could be addressed through probation and if the offender is willing to cooperate Availability of programmes, specialist group work, and intensive probation Where offending is less serious
Deferred Sentence	Mainly for those requiring drugs or alcohol counselling but who do not require the additional support of probation supervision

The majority of sheriffs indicated that the risk of re-offending and protection of the public interest and safety were key elements which they took into account when considering a custodial disposal. Although some sheriffs used custody as a deterrent, others considered that custody did not always deter offenders but that they would use custody to contain offenders who were a danger to the community. Most sheriffs were reluctant to use short custodial sentences as these were not seen as achieving a great deal, especially as there were other options now available.

Community service was not generally viewed by sheriffs to be suitable for sex offenders or for people with drugs or alcohol problems. Where the offender was motivated to change his/her behaviour and had experienced several custodial sentences, some sheriffs might try probation but would tend to request bi-monthly reports if the offender was classified as "high risk". Probation was seen by a few sheriffs as providing some control over the offender's behaviour, diminishing the risk of re-offending rather than expecting a "cure".

Some sheriffs were reluctant to impose deferred sentence with social work support because it could not be enforced. Other sheriffs said that, where necessary, they would maintain control by requesting bi-monthly reports, but not routinely as this was time-consuming for social workers. They indicated that this was, in some cases, preferable to a probation order where they would be unaware that the offender was not participating fully unless his/her behaviour warranted breach proceedings.

FACTORS WHICH INFLUENCE SER RECOMMENDATIONS

Social workers were asked to identify the factors which influenced a probation and a community service recommendation. Social workers tended to view community service as suitable for the more serious offences (including isolated offences) where there was a risk of custody. They added that offenders should have a stable home environment and be able and willing to work. Social workers said that they might recommend community service if the offender had rejected all previous social work supervision and/or denied responsibility for the offence (whereas some sheriffs suggested that such cases might receive a custodial sentence).

Social workers in each area indicated that they would recommend probation only if they identified issues connected with the offending which could be addressed and if the offender acknowledged this and was prepared to work on these issues. In two areas, where there were specialist projects available[12], social workers were prepared to recommend probation if the offender had a problem with violence. Sex offenders were not eligible for community service in Wallace[13] but social workers might recommend probation if such offenders accepted responsibility for their offence.

Deferred sentence was viewed by social workers as suitable for some offenders who did not have the personal resources to comply with the very structured regime of probation supervision. It was suggested that one of the benefits of deferred sentence was that the offender had to take responsibility for his/her own behaviour.

Social workers indicated that there was a variety of circumstances in which they might not be able to provide a recommendation for a community based disposal:

- if the offender was in prison for another offence;

- in Wallace, where sex offenders were not eligible for community service and they denied responsibility for their offence;

- for offenders who were considered by social workers to have committed "quite dangerous" offences, as social workers could not work with them because of personal safety issues;

- if all community disposals had been tried;

- if the offender refused to cooperate with, or was considered unsuitable for, community service or probation and could not afford to pay a fine.

Sheriffs and social workers tended to use similar criteria for suitability for community based disposals. However, as the National Standards were developed in consultation between social work interests and the judiciary, one would expect their criteria to be similar. Social work criteria were consistent with service objectives contained in the National Standards (which are summarised in Chapter Two).

---

12 In Wallace there was a specialist project to address violence and in Bruce, when probation is offered as an alternative to custody, social workers sometimes include anger management.
13 Social work department policy.

THE INFLUENCE OF THE SER

In addition to wider considerations, such as protection of the public interest or safety, sentencer decision making was found to be based on a complex combination of factors relating to the offence, the offender and social work services. Although the information presented in court would provide details of the offence, whether the offender had had previous experience of community based disposals and whether these had been breached, the SER assesses these factors within the offender's personal and social context. The SER is also the main source of information about factors relating to the offender, such as the existence of a problem which could be addressed through probation.

However, in cases where an SER is not requested and a custodial sentence is imposed, social workers do not have the opportunity to influence the sentencer's decision. The social work department can have little influence other than alerting sentencers through liaison as to how new initiatives and community disposals in general might be able to deal effectively with such offenders. In addition, those offenders who have been given a custodial sentence because community disposals had previously been tried, possibly before the recent improvements in probation supervision, may not have had an opportunity for high quality social work support. Social workers suggested that some older offenders might now benefit from a probation order having served several custodial sentences. However, they said that social workers were unable to assess these offenders as SERs tended to be requested for younger offenders:

> "It is not unusual to come across someone who has never been offered probation but who has had several custodial sentences or fines throughout his life - we'd love to have the opportunity of undertaking an assessment for probation." (Social Workers)

Although it would appear that sheriffs and social workers generally shared a common understanding of the criteria for suitability for different disposals, it is evident that social workers considered that some offenders given custody might have benefited from a community disposal. This suggests a need for further liaison between the judiciary and social work departments about priorities for requesting SERs[14] and the effectiveness of community based disposals. However, it is important to understand that although sentencers and social workers can work together, they have different roles and the sentencer has considerations other than the offender to take into account when sentencing.

CONCLUSION

One of the main aims of the policy is to reduce the use of custody by increasing the availability, improving the quality and targeting the use of community based court disposals on these most at risk of custody.

The views provided by sheriffs indicate that the availability and quality of community based disposals is only one aspect which they consider when deciding between custody and a community based disposal. Other considerations are taken into account, such as the need to protect the public interest or safety and factors relating to the offender, for example, their motivation to stop offending.

By focusing on the quality and availability of community based disposals social work is addressing some sentencing concerns. It is important to recognise this when assessing the impact of the policy.

---

[14] The inspection of SERs found that service managers said that they had not yet used the National Standards to discuss priorities for requesting SERs locally. The inspection obtained views from the judiciary, social work managers and social workers and analysed 443 SERs throughout Scotland. (*Helping the Court Decide: Report on an Inspection of Social Enquiry Reports for the Criminal Courts*, SWSI 1996.)

CHAPTER FOUR
THE SOCIAL ENQUIRY REPORT

INTRODUCTION

The previous chapter identified factors which influenced sentencing decisions. It was found that the social workers had an important role to play in providing information and assessments in the SER relating to these factors. The purpose of this chapter is thus to examine in more depth the type of information sought from the SER and whether this information was provided, and to explore the concept of "quality" of SERs and whether reports met the criteria of a good quality SER.

Comparisons are made between: the views of sentencers (seven sheriffs in total); those of social workers (one court social worker and a group of four social workers from each area); the guidance contained in the National Standards; and the information provided in reports in the SER sample (212 reports).[15]

INFORMATION SOUGHT IN THE SER

Sheriffs were asked to identify the key information which they sought in an SER and social workers were asked to identify the key information which they thought they should provide in the SER.

Their responses covered a wide range of topics. The categories most commonly identified are grouped into:

A. Those which were identified as key information by three or more sheriffs but were rarely identified as key information by social workers.

- Family background/social history.
- Employment.

B. Those which were identified as key information by three or more sheriffs and by three or more social workers.

- Pattern of offending.
- Reasons for offending.
- Prevention of further offending by an appropriate community disposal.

C. Those which were identified as key information by three or more social workers but rarely by sheriffs.

- Attitude to offence.
- Range of appropriate disposals and conclusions.

---

[15] As the SER sample is a quota and not a representative sample, any analysis can only relate to the Standards which have been met in the cases in the sample and cannot be applied to SERs in general.

STAFFORDSHIRE
UNIVERSITY
LIBRARY

The National Standards provide guidance to social workers about the information which should be provided in the SER. This information is referred to as "essential contents" and is summarised in Table 4.1.

Table 4.1: Summary of National Standards Essential Contents

Information relevant to offending	Circumstances surrounding offence Offending history Attitude to offence (cause, seriousness) How personal and social circumstances may have contributed to offending behaviour
Information relevant to sentence/disposal	Response to previous court disposals Income and financial commitments Family responsibilities, employment, housing which are relevant to disposal Resources available to assist/supervise offender in community Physical and mental health, including use of alcohol or other drugs
Review and conclusions	Review feasible community based options in light of re-offending, response to previous disposals and suitability for options reviewed Consequences of specific disposals, particularly custody Subject's needs associated with offending behaviour and resources to meet these Seriousness with which subject views offending behaviour/motivation to change
Recommendations	Feasible community based options Preferred option or reasons for no recommendation Probation: arrangements for supervision; objectives; action plan frequency of contact; indicate if additional requirements are necessary Community service: are circumstances sufficiently serious to indicate custody as the alternative; suitability of offender

It can be seen that the key information identified by three or more social workers focused on offending behaviour, which was consistent with the National Standards. Sheriffs also included "family background" and "employment" as key information which reflects the more traditional model of SER. However, most sheriffs explained that they sought this information to provide an indication of the cause of offending. The National Standards state that personal and social background information should be obtained and analysed to investigate and understand the possible reasons for the subject's offending behaviour. This is consistent with the sheriffs' views.

INFORMATION PROVIDED IN THE SER

Key Information

Table 4.2 shows the proportion of reports in each of the four samples which provided the key information identified by sheriffs and social workers.

Table 4.2: Key Information Provided in the SER

	Scott %	Wallace %	Burns %	Bruce %
A Identified by Mainly Sheriffs:				
Family background/social history	91	100	96	96
Employment	89	83	94	94
B Identified by Sheriffs and Social Workers:				
Pattern of offending	25	31	19	13
Reasons for offending	58	56	62	73
Prevention of further offending by appropriate community disposal	2	14	27	20
C Identified by Mainly Social Workers:				
Attitude to offence	51	71	73	76
Range of appropriate disposals and conclusions	98	96	98	96

The table shows that those categories identified as key information by mainly sheriffs were provided in most reports in the sample, despite social workers rarely identifying this as key information.

The key information identified both by sheriffs and social workers were, however, provided much less frequently in reports in the sample, with assessments of risk or prevention of further offending being least likely to be provided.

Although three or more social workers (but few sheriffs) identified "attitude to the offence" and "a range of appropriate disposals and conclusions" as key information, the former were not always provided in reports, most especially in Scott.

The National Standards Essential Contents

The reports in the SER sample were examined to assess the extent to which they provided the information described by the National Standards as "essential contents". The average proportion of "essential contents" provided in each area was: 66 per cent in Bruce; 68 per cent in Wallace; 70 per cent in Burns; and 71 per cent in Scott. There are 25 categories of National Standards 'essential contents'. Table 4.3 shows those categories where less than 60 per cent of reports in at least one of the four study areas provided this information.

Table 4.3: Proportion of Reports in Sample Providing Selected* Essential Contents

*Categories where less than 60 per cent of reports in at least one area provided information

	Scott %	Wallace %	Burns %	Bruce %
Information Relevant to Offending:				
Attitude to offence	51	71	65	60
Circumstances contributing to offending behaviour	68	44	58	40
Information Relevant to Sentence/Disposal:				
Response to previous disposals	54	69	69	67
Mental Health	28	54	52	20
Physical Health	81	81	85	56
SER Review and Conclusion: Risk of re-offending	2	14	27	20
Consequences of disposal for offender/family	16	44	33	22
Needs of offender/resources to be used	32	15	42	35
Offender's view of seriousness of offence	19	4	17	20
Motivation to change	40	27	33	29
Probation Recommendation Frequency of contact	0	0	0	0
Offender understands implication of order	35	26	35	40
CS Recommendation: Suitability for CS	55	53	75	70

It is interesting to note that, although there was little variation between courts in respect of all of the "essential contents", there was some variation between courts in the extent to which specific items of information were covered. Table 4.3 relates only to those items which were covered by 60 per cent or less of reports in at least one area. It shows that in the sample of reports, no individual area consistently had a low coverage of "essential contents".

None of the reports in the sample provided information on the proposed frequency of contact in cases where probation was recommended. The section in which reports were least likely to provide information was the SER review and conclusion. Within this section, assessments of risk of re-offending and the offender's view of the seriousness of the offence were least likely to be provided. The SWSI inspection of SERs in Scotland (SWSI, 1996) found that exploration of offending behaviour was found to be particularly weak and that 47 per cent of their sample provided an assessment of risk of re-offending. One of the inspection's conclusions was that:

> "We think that the subject of offending behaviour is central to the preparation of reports.... The challenge for the service is how to improve the quality of this information and advice." (SWSI, 1996, p.19)

IMPLICATIONS OF MISSING INFORMATION

It would appear that social workers still provided information relevant to the traditional model of report writing which gave more descriptive information such as family background and personal circumstances, rather than how these contributed to offending behaviour and other assessments of offending behaviour (requiring analysis rather than description), which the Standards now advocate. However, social workers did identify information relating to offending behaviour as key information. There would thus appear to be a discrepancy between what information they thought they *should provide* and what information they *provided in practice*.

Reasons for Missing Information

It cannot be concluded that the absence of information indicated that the social worker did not obtain this information. Social workers reported that they obtained a wide range of information when preparing the SER but often included only relevant information in the report. This view was consistent with the findings of the inspection (SWSI, 1996). Both sheriffs and courts social workers considered that it was not necessary to include all the "essential contents" as they were not always relevant to the individual case. However, it was suggested by court social workers that the "essential contents" broad headings should be covered:

> "Some mention should be made under each heading because we're still at the stage of needing the structure of the National Standards in order to feel that we've adequately covered everything." (Court Social Worker)

Social workers reported that they were frequently unable to provide an assessment of the pattern of offending as they often had problems in obtaining access to the Scottish Criminal Records Office full list of previous convictions. (The procurators fiscal often selected previous convictions to libel in court on the basis of relevance.)

The need for assessment of risk of self-harm, harm to others or of mental health, was considered by sheriffs and practitioners to be very infrequent. Sheriffs said that they tended to receive an assessment of risk of self-harm or harm to others where relevant and where these were provided they found them to be helpful in alerting the sheriff to the need for a psychiatric report for an assessment of whether probation on a condition of outpatient treatment would be appropriate.

Risk of Re-offending

All sheriffs said that they only occasionally received an assessment of the risk of re-offending in the SER (consistent with the results of the sample) but when they did, they found this assessment helpful. Where this information was not provided, most sheriffs thought that they could extract this assessment from the information provided in the report. Sheriffs disagreed about the most appropriate disposal where there was a risk of re-offending. One sheriff assumed that a recommendation for a community based social work disposal implied that there was a risk of re-offending, whereas another sheriff would impose custody if such a risk existed. As the existence of risk of re-offending can, for some sentencers, be a factor in the decision to impose a custodial sentence, and for others, a central consideration of sentencing, it is important that this assessment is explicitly addressed in the SER.

There was found to be some discrepancy between the views of some sheriffs and the guidance provided in the National Standards regarding the role of the social worker in making assessments of risk of re-offending. The Standards state that report writers should consider a range of indicators associated with the risk of further offending and that they should assess which disposal might be most constructive from the point of view of avoiding or reducing future offending behaviour. However, some sheriffs thought that such an assessment was difficult for social workers to undertake as the offender can "pull the wool over the eyes of the social worker" and that the sheriff was in a better position to make an assessment of risk of re-offending. Views obtained from sheriffs during the inspection (SWSI, 1996) also found that sheriffs tended to rely on their own experience when assessing the risk of re-offending and the offender's motivation to change.

Probation Action Plan

Sheriffs indicated that most reports with a probation recommendation did have an action plan but if this was missing, they might ask for a supplementary report. When asked what information they looked for in an action plan, sheriffs listed the following: the problem to be addressed; how to tackle the problem; frequency of contact (especially for borderline cases); level of monitoring; goals and time-scale. Sheriffs acknowledged that although many reports might say what they were hoping to achieve, they did not necessarily set out the detail of the programme as it was sometimes not possible to provide details at that stage.

Contrary to the sheriffs' views, some court social workers thought that there did not need to be a great deal of detail in the action plan, and that methods to be used and frequency of contact were not sought by sheriffs, unless it was a serious offence and a high risk was involved. As court social workers did not identify a need to include frequency of contact this may partly explain why reports did not provide this information. They suggested that social workers did not have the time to go into a lot of detail at the SER stage but that a full action plan was developed as part of the initial process of probation.

The Standards suggest that the SER action plan should contain as much information as possible but they recognise that sometimes it is not always realistic to do so at that stage. It would thus appear that there was some confusion about the detail of SER action plans between the guidance contained in the Standards, sheriffs' views and social workers' understanding of the level of detail which sheriffs sought.

Although it would appear that sheriffs and social workers, to a certain extent, shared an understanding of the key information which should be provided in the SER, there was some discrepancy between what was identified as key information, the information provided in the reports in the SER sample and the information which the Standards consider to be "essential contents". To explore this further, a comparison is made about the overall quality of SERs between the guidance in the Standards and the views of sheriffs and court social workers.

THE QUALITY OF SOCIAL ENQUIRY REPORTS

Criteria of Quality

Sheriffs and court social workers were asked to identify the criteria they would use to describe a good quality SER. Comparisons were made between their views and the "ground rules" for preparing SERs, contained in the National Standards[16]. The "ground rules" can be viewed as providing a general indication of the quality of reports and are summarised below:

1. Reports must be written clearly and concisely.

2. Reports must be logical and well argued with conclusions and recommendations flowing from the main body of the report.

3. Reports must set out the basis on which they are prepared including the numbers of contacts with the offender and others.

4. Care must be taken to distinguish clearly fact from opinion and surmise.

5. There is no need to repeat factual information which is known to be available to the court from other sources.

6. When writing SERs care must be taken to avoid using phrases which imply moral judgements and which tend to label or stereotype offenders.

7. Reports should balance positives and negatives.

8. SERs must always refer to the offender's physical and mental health.

9. The aim of the report is to assist the court's consideration of whether community based options are appropriate.

Sheriffs and court social workers shared similar views on the criteria of a good quality SER and their responses covered some of the National Standards ground rules: full information; information required for a decision on disposal; concise and readable; and recommendations and conclusions clearly evidenced.

Sheriffs mentioned criteria relating to both information and style of writing as being consistent with a good quality SER, whereas court social workers tended to refer to the style of writing. Although three sheriffs welcomed full information and did not object to a long report, as they would disregard superfluous information, some court social workers considered that a long report did not necessarily indicate a better report and that the chances of the sheriff reading it all were very slim. One of these court social workers said:

> "It's not always the case that longer means better or that you are better informed, its more that you're able to use the information effectively and be confident of your assessment in using what is necessary to paint a picture of the person." (Court Social Worker)

---

[16] The National Standards, 1991. SER section, paragraph 71.

Another court social worker emphasised that a good quality report was one when:

> "...at the end of the report I feel I really know the person and their circumstances, the conclusion seems appropriate and it's not just going through all the headings in the Standards rather laboriously or mechanically."

(Court Social Worker)

Quality of Reports

Sheriffs' Views

All sheriffs said that the majority of reports met their definition of good quality and that the general standard of SERs had always been high. Sheriffs were not aware of any overall changes in the quality of SERs since the implementation of the policy but some did acknowledge that they had improved in certain aspects, as they now tended to include: an action plan; an assessment of attitude to the offence and victim awareness; and were generally better structured. (However, it was previously noted that, apart from the objectives of probation, details of the action plan were rarely provided.)

However, many sheriffs interviewed in 1993 in Phase One (McAra 1998) identified major improvements in SER writing, especially in respect of the recommendations and conclusions. Views of sheriffs obtained by the inspection (SWSI 1996) showed that most sheriffs considered that the quality of SERs had improved since the introduction of the National Standards.

In this study a sheriff from Bruce suggested that, as the standard of report writing had been "sharpened up" rather than dramatically improved (because it was already of a high standard), he would have greater confidence, in borderline cases, that the community based disposal would be thoroughly supervised and administered. One Wallace sheriff suggested that the social workers were "working up to the Standards" before they came into effect and this was confirmed by the social workers. Scott social workers also said that they had been working to senior management guidelines prior to 1991 and that these did not differ much from the Standards.

Social Workers' Views

Most court social workers considered that, as a result of the Standards, SERs had improved, for example, they were now: more structured; more focused on offending behaviour and pattern of offending rather than on family and personal background (although Table 4.2 showed that this was not the case in relation to the SER sample); included an action plan; and covered every section identified in the Standards, whereas before the Standards, they considered that such information was sometimes omitted or covered only briefly. The court social workers believed that assessments of the risk of re-offending were now generally undertaken well and that this assessment was usually undertaken prior to the standards (except in Burns). However, this assessment was rarely provided in the reports in our sample. It would thus appear that court social workers aligned quality with National Standards guidance. Court social workers and managers considered that in addition to the introduction of the National Standards, the quality of SERs had also improved as a result of the shift to specialisation when social workers gained more experience and expertise in the preparation of reports.

Although court social workers and social work managers acknowledged that there had been improvements, they identified certain areas where further improvements could be made, for example, by taking a more analytic approach rather than being descriptive[17]. A more in-depth analysis was seen to be required when assessing the offender's attitude to the offence and they considered that the action plan could be more dynamic and unique to the particular offender. A need for further training was identified in relation to assessments of mental illness and risk of self-harm. Social workers acknowledged that most specialist workers produced good quality reports but that there were certain constraints which operated occasionally.

Constraints on Providing a Good Quality SER

Availability of Information

In some circumstances social workers were unable to provide a good quality report because of the lack of information. For example, the main information on the offence which the social worker received was the

---

[17] This view was consistent with that of the Inspection. (SWSI, 1996).

complaint (the charge and basic details of the offence) which did not provide a detailed account of the circumstances surrounding the offence. Occasionally social workers received feedback from the court social worker on information presented to the court or they sometimes referred to media reports of a trial. Their assessment of attitude to the offence was therefore mainly based on an analysis of the offender's perception of the offence. Sheriffs, social workers and managers recognised that without accurate details of the offence, the author of the SER was unable to challenge or validate the offender's version of events. As one sheriff suggested:

> "The social workers can only repeat what the offender says, he is at the mercy of his client - therefore the narrative can be totally at odds with what is said in court. It sounds like a plea in mitigation." (Sheriff)

Social workers emphasised that it was essential in terms of assessments for community based disposals that authors of SERs had full details of the offence and the effect on the victim. The accused often minimised the offence (the account given by the procurator fiscal could, for example, refer to more violence than that provided by the offender). In terms of accountability or assessing the offender's willingness to take responsibility for the offence, it was essential that social workers obtained detailed information about the offence to assess the offender's level of commitment as a potential probationer. Social workers reported that if they had to rely on the offender's version alone, there was a danger that their assessment for community based disposals could become inappropriate and be viewed by sheriffs as unrealistic. Social workers indicated that they would welcome access to witness statements and police reports (as occurs in England in the preparation of pre-sentence reports). The inspection (SWSI, 1996) acknowledged that there was a need to consider appropriate steps to be taken to increase the information given to practitioners about the current offence and its impact on the victim. Managers reported that procurators fiscal tended to be reluctant to provide this information on a routine basis and they compared this with the arrangements in respect of diversion where procurators fiscal provided full information.

Other Reasons

Other reasons which sheriffs and court social workers attributed to the occasional poor reports were:

- pressure of work (especially during holiday periods; workers in split posts being called away to undertake emergency child protection work).

- lack of time (administrative delays in processing the request and sending notification of an appointment to the offender; incorrect address given).

- they had been prepared by a social worker from another area or by generic social workers who tended to provide a lot of information on family background and personal details. Although generic workers had not received the same level of training on preparation of reports as specialist workers, court social workers considered that they could provide a different dimension to their assessment, having had prolonged contact with the offender in another area of work.

- delays in accessing other agencies. (There was found to be a particular difficulty in contacting the relevant psychiatrist.)

Social workers said they generally attempted to follow up the first interview in the office with a second interview at home, if they had time, when the family could be seen and information corroborated. A second interview was considered desirable in a high profile case or when there was a high risk of custody. However, if there was an issue about the social worker's safety or if there was not sufficient time, only one interview was undertaken, usually in the office. Over two-thirds of reports in the sample involved one interview with the offender and 40 per cent involved contact with the offender's family. Social workers suggested that the quality of some reports suffered when only one interview was undertaken, as did the inspection (SWSI, 1996), but that it was not considered essential in each case and would have been impracticable for every SER.

By the spring of 1995, two of the four study courts (Burns and Bruce) had extended the length of time within which SERs were to be submitted to 21 days for those on remand and 28 days for those in the community. However, some visiting sheriffs in these courts did not apply the extended time-scale. Sheriffs in the remaining courts resisted the extension as they did not consider an extra week's delay to be fair on the offender, but they did acknowledge the pressure which this imposed on social workers whom they considered had coped reasonably well. Although it was suggested that insufficient time to prepare SERs sometimes resulted in a poor quality report, Gelsthorpe and Raynor (1995)[18] found that in England, the average quality of short-notice reports did not differ significantly from the average quality of other reports.

---

[18] Gelsthorpe, L. and Raynor, P. (1995) Quality and Effectiveness in Probation Officers' Reports to Sentencers. *The British Journal of Criminology,* 35, 2, 188-199.

In parts of Scott, requests to substance misuse services for information for an SER were not prioritised and the social worker was unlikely to obtain the information by the time the report was due. Similarly, in Burns, social workers were unlikely to receive an assessment from alcohol counselling services in time to include this in the report. In Scott and Burns, requests to the procurator fiscal about pending cases or warrants were required to be made in writing and there were sometimes difficulties in obtaining this information in time to complete the report for court.

Improving the Quality of Reports

All research areas had introduced monitoring procedures since the introduction of the National Standards to ensure that SERs were consistent with the guidance contained in the Standards. In each area, prior to the court hearing, the court social worker proof-checked the majority of reports and ensured that the basic information was provided. In three areas the court social worker had devised a monitoring form on which they noted whether certain information and assessments had been provided but the content of these forms varied.

Scott and Burns:	Monitoring forms were detailed and they collected information on the "essential contents" - but with a focus on descriptive details rather than whether a more analytic approach had been taken. Additional overall comments relating to clarity, the argument and whether a complete picture of the person was provided.
Bruce:	Three headings related to whether reports were: concise and relevant; focused on offending behaviour; and had credible conclusions and recommendations.

In the larger courts a sample of SERs were examined by local court social workers and/or managers and results sent to managers and ultimately to social workers. In the smaller court (Bruce) all SERs were examined and results were submitted to managers. Training sessions were arranged with social workers if particular areas of reports were found to be inadequate. It is thus evident that there was some variation in the extent to which SERs were monitored and the methods used. However, each area was committed to improving the quality of SERs.

CONCLUSION

As seen in the previous chapter, the SER has an important role to play in assisting sentencers to decide between custody and a community based disposal. It is thus important that the quality of SERs is high to facilitate the policy objective of a reduction in the use of custody.

Sheriffs generally considered that the quality of SERs was sufficient. Nevertheless, it was found that there were some gaps in provision of the key information which sheriffs sought in the SER. Difficulties in obtaining information from procurators fiscal and agencies often inhibited the preparation of a good quality report. Court social workers and social work managers also recognised that there was scope for further improvement in the preparation of SERs.

The potential of the social work contribution to sentencing decisions was thus not fully achieved at the time of the research.

STAFFORDSHIRE UNIVERSITY LIBRARY

CHAPTER FIVE
SENTENCING DECISIONS

INTRODUCTION

Previous chapters have examined the impact of the policy on sentencing decisions by obtaining views of sheriffs and social work practitioners about changes they have perceived in the quality and content of SERs and by examining the extent to which reports in the SER sample met the National Standards. These can be viewed as indicators of social work practice. Indicators of sentencing practice include factors influencing sentencing decisions (discussed in Chapter Three), sentencing trends and conversion of SER recommendation to disposal.

This chapter examines the impact of the policy on sentencing decisions by firstly examining sentencing trends relating to the period before and after introduction of the policy and factors which influence sentencing trends. SER recommendations and outcomes are compared and the factors which might have impacted on the level of conversion of recommendations are examined to assist an understanding of sentencer decision making.

SENTENCING TRENDS

Factors Influencing Sentencing Trends

There are many factors which can influence sentencing trends and thus it is difficult to isolate the impact of the policy from other factors. Factors unrelated to the policy might include an increase in the incidence of more serious offences, legislative changes, and the high level of use of temporary sheriffs in some areas. Although temporary sheriffs have access to literature on local specialist services, contact with court social workers is hindered as temporary sheriffs tend not to be allocated to the same court on a regular basis.

In addition, the introduction of a new policy requires a considerable period before a clear impact is likely to be identified. In relation to this policy, the reorganisation to specialist structures within social work departments, the introduction of specialist initiatives, and the requirement to meet National Standards, involved considerable changes. The process of policy implementation is thus likely to be gradual and to extend over a number of years before full implementation can be achieved. This view is supported by the findings of the probation study (McIvor and Barry, 1998) which showed that social work departments had not fully implemented the National Standards by the end of the fieldwork in early summer 1995. It is expected that the gradual process of policy implementation would be reflected in sentencing decisions. An analysis of sentencing trends to the end of 1994 can thus only provide an indication of the impact of the policy on sentencing decisions in the early years of implementation.

Achievement of changes in sentencing attitudes and decisions would also be expected to be a gradual process. Sabol (1990)[19], in his discussion of the impact of the policy on the use of fines, also argued that changes in policy are insufficient on their own to change sentencing outcomes.

> "The uncertainty surrounding a new policy diminishes the likelihood that it will be adopted without other forms of support or justification. Further, if outcomes are viewed as indicative of the preferences of sentencers, then over the long run those preferences have changed slowly even in the face of new penal policies or a multitude of criminal justice acts". (Page 26).

> "There is not a mechanistic relationship between penal policy and the responses or decisions of sentencers. Only after the relevant information produced a diminution in uncertainty about their effectiveness did fine use increase steadily and finally rapidly." (Page 34).

The following graphs are based on the proportion of all charges proved in sheriff courts in Scotland and in each of the study courts from 1989 to 1994 (Scottish Office criminal justice statistics)[20]. The figures upon which the graphs and discussion of this section are based can be found in the tables in Annex III.

---

[19] Sabol, W.J. (1990) "Improvement, Fines and Diverting Offenders from Custody: Implications of Sentencing Discretion for Penal Policy", *The Howard Journal*, 29, 1, 25-41.

[20] These statistics have been provided by criminal justice statisticians from The Scottish Office Home Department and have not previously been published in this form. There have been technical difficulties with The Scottish Office criminal justice statistics for 1991. These statistics are currently being reviewed and amended statistics will be available in 1998. It is expected that the proportionate use of custody and community service for 1991 will then be slightly higher than the figures presented in this report. However, this is not likely to significantly affect the trends identified in the following discussion.

The Use of Custody

All Age Groups

Figure 1 shows the changes in the use of custody in each of the study courts and in sheriff courts in Scotland as a whole between 1989 and 1994.

The proportion of cases given custody in sheriff courts in Scotland, although decreasing slightly in 1991, showed an increase since introduction of the policy from 11 per cent in 1991 to 15 per cent in 1994. This pattern was reflected in Burns, although there was a slight decrease in 1994. Scott has followed the national trend though with a slightly steeper increase. The proportion given custody in Bruce and Wallace fluctuated over this period but increased by three per cent in Wallace in 1994. Scott and Wallace tended to have a higher use of custody than Scotland during this period, whilst Bruce and Burns tended to be lower than the national figure.

Figure 1: Use of Custody

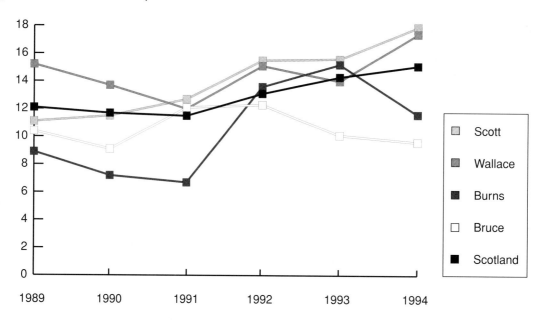

It would appear that there was not a reduction in the use of custody after implementation of the policy. However, the sheriffs in Wallace and Bruce said in interview that they were not really surprised that there had been little change in the use of custody in their courts because the standard of social work services to the courts had been very high both before and after policy implementation.

As seen in Chapter Three, the gravity of the offence was considered to be a major factor influencing sentencers' decisions on whether or not to impose a custodial sentence. If the proportion of serious offences which might attract a custodial sentence had increased since 1991, then any reduction in the use of custody as a result of the policy would be masked. For example, sheriffs from Bruce and Scott had noted an increase in the number of housebreakings which they said would tend to attract a prison sentence. However, Scottish Office statistics did not identify an increase in Bruce (Table II, Annex III). In Scott, although there was a decrease in 1990 and 1991 after which levels increased to that of 1989 and 1990, the number of people being convicted for housebreaking as a proportion of all crimes and offences did increase from 1992. There was, however, an increase in the use of custody for housebreaking in each of these courts.

The court social worker from Scott considered that crimes had been becoming more serious and that there had been an increase in organised crime. A Scott sheriff had also noted an increase in car thefts and carrying weapons (as a result, a campaign had been mounted against the latter). Although the statistics showed that there had been an increase in handling weapons in Scott since 1991, the level returned to that prior to 1991. In Wallace, where a campaign had also been introduced, there was a decrease in handling weapons in 1990 and this level was maintained until 1994 when it increased. The statistics confirmed that there had been an increase in the use of custody from 1992 in Scott and from 1993 in Wallace. The increase in incidence would suggest that the use of custody in these courts as a deterrent for handling weapons had not been totally effective.

Although The Scottish Office statistics do not provide information on gravity of offences, the statistics (Table III, Annex III) show that throughout Scotland, there had been an increase in the incidence and rate per 1,000 crimes of persons convicted of handling weapons (most noticeably after the implementation of the policy in 1991). However, the proportion of those given a custodial sentence for theft of a motor vehicle, housebreaking and handling weapons increased, most markedly since 1991, the first year of implementation of the policy. Although the gravity of these particular crimes could have increased, it appears that sheriffs throughout Scotland were more likely to impose a custodial sentence for these crimes since 1991.

Under 21 Age Group

Although we have seen that the use of custody in Scotland had increased slightly since 1991, this might not have been reflected in all age groups. One of the objectives of the policy was to target the use of community based disposals on those most at risk of custody, especially young adult repeat offenders. If the policy had impacted on sentencing in the early years, one would expect to see a decrease in the use of custody in the younger age-groups. Table 5.1 shows the use of custody for those aged under 21 as a proportion of all charges proved in each sheriff court.

Table 5.1: Proportionate Use of Custody for Offenders Aged Under 21

	Scott %	Wallace %	Burns %	Bruce %	Scotland %
1989	14	20	11	13	15
1990	13	19	10	15	14
1991	13	17	10	18	14
1992	16	19	17	16	16
1993	18	20	23	16	17
1994	19	23	9	13	18

In the under 21 age group, there was a very slight increase in the use of custody in Scotland as a whole between 1992 and 1994. However, there was a marked increase in the use of custody for this age group in Burns where the proportion of under 21s receiving a custodial sentence increased dramatically from ten per cent in 1991 to 23 per cent by the end of 1993 (which is contrary to the expectations of the policy), but decreased to nine per cent in 1994.

In Bruce, there was a slight increase in the use of custody for this age group in 1991 but the level returned to that of previous years. In Wallace, there was a decrease in the use of custody for the under 21s in 1991 but increased since then to a level slightly higher than that of 1989. In Scott, there had been a gradual increase since 1992, which one sheriff thought might be due to an increase in car thefts, housebreaking and carrying of weapons by offenders. In 1994, Wallace had the highest use of custody for this age group.

21 to 25 Age Group

Table 5.2 shows the use of custody for those aged between 21 and 25 as a proportion of all charges proved in each sheriff court.

Table 5.2: Proportionate Use of Custody for Offenders Aged 21 to 25

	Scott %	Wallace %	Burns %	Bruce %	Scotland %
1989	13	21	14	15	16
1990	16	18	9	10	15
1991	18	14	9	13	14
1992	21	19	16	16	16
1993	18	16	17	8	17
1994	25	20	15	12	18

For the 21 to 25 age group, the proportion given custody increased slightly in Scotland but fluctuated in Wallace and Bruce between 1989 and 1994. In Burns, (as in the younger age group) there was a marked increase in the use of custody in 1991 which was maintained thereafter but may reflect the level of use in 1989 and earlier. Scott showed a steady increase from 1989 to 1994 with a slight decrease in 1993.

Despite the aims of the policy, it would appear that there had not been a decreasing trend in the proportion of those given a custodial sentence since 1991 for those aged under 21 or between 21 and 25. If, however, there had been an increase in the incidence of more serious crimes and offences which would attract a longer custodial sentence, then this might have counterbalanced a reduction in the use of short custodial sentences for the less serious offences.

Short Custodial Sentences

Table 5.3 shows the proportion of those given short custodial sentences in sheriff courts in the study areas and in Scotland. (Table IV in Annex III provides the figures for all lengths of custodial sentence).

Table 5.3: Proportionate Use of Short Custodial Sentences

	1989 %	1990 %	1991 %	1992 %	1993 %	1994 %
Up to One Month						
Scott	18	21	15	15	14	11
Wallace	32	30	34	24	23	16
Burns	14	13	13	19	14	13
Bruce	12	10	12	8	12	4
Scotland	15	15	15	14	13	10
>1 to 3 Months						
Scott	49	45	45	45	42	37
Wallace	50	46	38	50	49	46
Burns	46	45	51	50	46	41
Bruce	59	64	57	55	53	47
Scotland	49	47	46	46	45	43

It is evident that there has been a decrease in the use of custodial sentences of up to one month in sheriff courts in Scotland since 1991, most noticeably in 1994. There was however a more dramatic drop in the proportion receiving this length of sentence in Scott in 1991 and in Wallace in 1992 and there has been a decrease in both areas since then. The figures for Burns and Bruce fluctuated from 1989.

For sentences over one month up to three months there was a gradual decrease in both Scotland and Scott from 1989 (and in Bruce, although there was an increase in 1990) which thus cannot be attributed to the impact of the policy. In Wallace and Burns the proportions fluctuated between 1989 and 1994.

It would thus appear that the policy might have had a marginal impact on the use of very short custodial sentences in Scotland and more markedly in two of the study courts. In interview, sheriffs indicated that they were not aware of having changed their use of short custodial sentences since the introduction of the policy. Some sheriffs considered that short sentences were not effective as little could be achieved in a short period of time.

It is interesting to note that the use of custodial sentences of up to one month in Wallace was much higher than in Scotland and the other study courts (in particular up to 1993). If the policy is directed towards the reduction of short custodial sentences of up to three months (as opposed to up to one month), it cannot be said to have been totally successful as over half of all those given custody in sheriff courts in Scotland and almost two-thirds of those in Wallace, continued to receive a short custodial sentence in 1994.

As the overall use of custody has increased slightly in Scotland since the introduction of the policy, then the proportionate use of one or more community based disposals must have decreased. The following sections attempt to identify where this may have occurred.

The Use of Probation

Figure 2 shows the changes in the use of probation in each of the study courts and in Scotland as a whole between 1989 and 1994.

Figure 2: Use of Probation

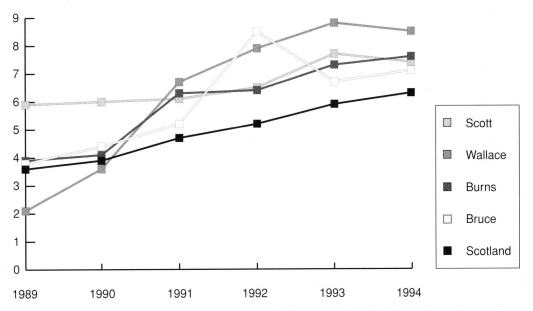

The proportion of cases given probation in Scotland as a whole increased slightly from almost four per cent in 1990 to six per cent in 1993, which could perhaps be related to the impact of the policy. The courts in our sample also showed an increase in the use of probation. In Wallace there was a gradual increase from two per cent in 1989 to over eight per cent in 1993. There was a slight increase in Scott in 1993 and in Burns in 1991 and 1993. In Bruce the proportion increased from four per cent in 1989 to six per cent in 1994 with a sudden increase to eight per cent in 1992.

Since 1991, all of the study courts had a slightly higher use of probation than for Scotland as a whole. These figures would tend to suggest that the policy has had a limited impact on the use of probation overall. However, the policy was targeted at young adult offenders in particular. Table 5.4 shows the use of probation for young offenders as a proportion of all charges proved in each sheriff court.

Table 5.4: Proportionate Use Of Probation For Young Offenders 1989-1994

	Scott %	Wallace %	Burns %	Bruce %	Scotland %
Aged under 21					
1989	10	4	9	7	6
1990	11	6	6	7	7
1991	9	15	10	9	8
1992	10	17	10	15	9
1993	13	19	11	11	10
1994	14	16	13	16	11
Aged 21 to 25					
1989	4	1	3	3	3
1990	4	3	4	4	3
1991	4	4	6	2	4
1992	4	4	6	9	4
1993	6	4	7	8	5
1994	4	6	8	5	5

It can be seen that probation was more often used for those aged under 21 than those aged 21 to 25. For the 21 to 25 age group, there was only a marginal increase of two per cent in the use of probation between 1989 and 1994 for Scotland as a whole. In Bruce and Scott, the use of probation fluctuated whereas there was an increase of five per cent in Wallace and Burns during this period. These increasing trends were evident prior to 1991 and thus cannot be wholly attributed to the policy.

In the under 21 age group, there was a gradual increase in Scotland between 1989 and 1994. In three of the study courts, there was an increase of between four per cent and nine per cent and in Wallace an increase of 12 per cent during this period. However, in Scott, Wallace and Bruce there was a more noticeable increase since policy implementation. In Wallace, this occurred in 1991 compared to 1992 in Bruce and 1993 in Scott, perhaps because reorganisation to a specialist structure took place earlier in Wallace than the other courts. However, the Wallace sheriffs suggested that the increase in 1991 coincided with the introduction of intensive probation projects. The level of use of probation for this age group was much higher in Wallace in 1993 than in the other courts under study, although in 1994 the use of custody was similar amongst three of the study courts. All of the study courts had a higher proportionate use of probation than Scotland as a whole, since 1991.

Most sheriffs indicated that they were more likely to use probation since the introduction of intensive probation projects and because probation had attained a higher credibility since the introduction of the National Standards, as it was better structured, more clearly focused and more thoroughly supervised. Another possible explanation for the slight increases in the use of probation was the introduction of section 7 orders which allows community service to be imposed as a condition of a probation order. There is, therefore, some evidence to suggest that the policy might have impacted on the use of probation, most especially in the under 21 age group in the study courts but less so in Scotland. The increase in the use of custody does therefore not appear to be related to any decrease in the use of probation.

Use of Community Service

Figure 3 opposite shows the proportion of cases given community service in each of the study courts and for Scotland as a whole. Although the rate for Scotland remained relatively stable between 1989 and 1994, the proportions in Wallace and Burns fluctuated during this period. However, in Bruce there was a slight increase in 1991 but has decreased since then to a lower level than 1989. In Scott there was a gradual increase in 1991 and 1992, a slight decrease in 1993, and increased again in 1994. Wallace and Bruce tended to be slightly higher than the average for Scotland, whereas Scott and Burns tended to be similar to the national average.

Figure 3: Use of Community Service

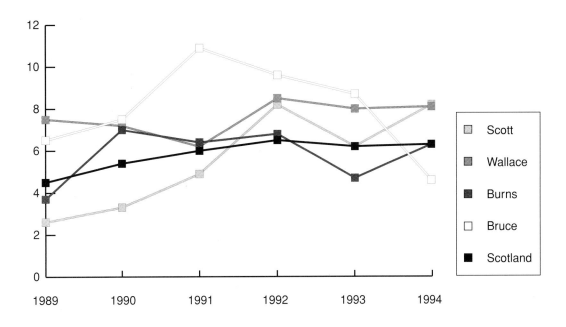

Although these figures would suggest that the policy has not had much impact on the use of community service, it should be noted that National Standards for community service were introduced in 1989. One sheriff suggested that there would only be a change in the use of community service if there was a change in the pattern of crime, which he thought had not occurred. Having noted an increase in the use of probation and not much change in the use of community service, one would therefore expect the increase in the use of custody to be balanced by a decrease in the use of fines.

The Use of Fines

Figure 4 shows that there has been a steady decrease in the use of fines since 1989 in Scotland as a whole and in Burns and Wallace. The overall trend in Scott and Bruce has also been declining with a slight increase in 1993 but decreasing again in 1994.

Figure 4: Use of Fines

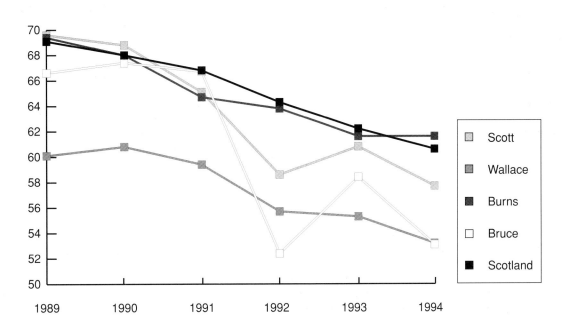

SER RECOMMENDATION AND DISPOSAL

The sentencing trends showed that the proportion of cases given custody in Scotland as a whole and in the study areas had increased between 1991 and 1994, contrary to the expectations of the policy. However, there was some evidence to suggest that the policy had impacted positively on the use of short custodial sentences and on the use of probation. In this section the differences between the SER recommendation and the disposal are explored to assist our understanding of these sentencing trends.

Level of Conversion in the Sample

It should be noted that, as we explained in Chapter One, our sample was a quota rather than a representative sample. The results should therefore not be taken as being representative of all reports in the study areas. Curran and Chambers[21] found an overall level of agreement of 69 per cent between SER recommendation and disposal in Scotland in 1976[22]. Our findings were similar with an overall level of conversion of 65 per cent, although the level of agreement varied between study courts: 77 per cent in Scott; 73 per cent in Bruce; 62 per cent in Burns; and 42 per cent in Wallace.

When exploring reasons for the low level of conversion of recommendation to disposal in Wallace, it was found that most of the community service recommendations which were rejected (8 out of 10 cases) received a custodial sentence. Most of those in Wallace whose probation recommendation was rejected (12 cases), received either custody (six) or community service (four). The Wallace sample had more previous convictions and greater previous experience of custody than other areas. The sample could thus be said to consist of "higher tariff" offenders who were at greater risk of custody than those offenders in the samples from the other research areas.

Half of the "no recommendations" in the sample received a custodial sentence. Cases with a "no recommendation" were more likely to result in custody in Wallace than in other courts (8 out of a total of 10 cases compared to between 2 and 5 in other courts) but the number of cases is very small. The social workers from Wallace indicated that they often used "no recommendation" for those offenders for whom they considered custody the most appropriate disposal. There was some indication that sheriffs acknowledged this.

Factors Influencing Acceptance of SER Recommendations

There is a range of factors which might influence levels of conversion. Carter and Wilkins[23] identified four possible explanations for conversion of recommendation to disposal: (i) the court's high regard for social workers' professional advice; (ii) the obviousness of the outcome; (iii) the social worker's ability to anticipate disposal; and (iv) a similar analysis of the situation by the court and social worker. Our study also identified these and a number of other reasons why SER recommendations might be followed by the sentencer:

Criteria for Suitability for Community Disposals are Shared

Although social workers and sheriffs tended, on the whole, to use similar criteria when considering suitability for community disposals, there were certain circumstances where they did not agree. For example, one sheriff from Wallace said that social workers might recommend probation for offenders committing serious offences which he considered was inappropriate. Social workers indicated that some sheriffs considered community service for cases where there was no risk of custody and that they would not recommend this disposal unless as an alternative to custody. Several sheriffs suggested that one reason for recommendations not being followed was that the sheriff had to take other matters into account, such as the gravity of the offence, offending patterns (although social workers should also consider such factors in their recommendation) and media pressure when there had been a spate of the same type of offence. In such cases they might impose custody to protect the public interest, but in some of these cases the SER recommendation might be probation or community service. One sheriff from Scott said that:

> "Social workers tend to recommend community service for carrying of knives and supply of drugs, but we are clamping down on these types of offences and impose a custodial sentence because it is a serious problem. However, if it is a first offender there may be some feature in a report that persuades me to use a community disposal". (Sheriff)

---

[21] Curran, J. H. and Chambers, G. A. (1982) *Social Enquiry Reports in Scotland.* A Scottish Office Social Research Study. HMSO.

[22] All SERs completed during a one month period in two regions were examined (180 reports).

[23] Carter, R. M. and Wilkins, L. T. (1967) 'Some Factors in Sentencing Policy'. *The Journal of Criminal Law, Criminology and Police Science* 58, 4. 503-514.

The Quality of Reports

If the definition of a good quality SER is regarded as one which provides the "essential contents" listed in the National Standards, it was found that quality was not related to whether or not the recommendation was followed. (There was no difference in the level of missing information between reports where the recommendation was accepted or rejected.) Although the number in the Gelsthorpe and Raynor sample was low, their findings suggested that:

> "Better reports were more successful in enabling sentencers to pass community sentences with confidence and to rely correspondingly less on imprisonment". (1995: p.197)

Court social workers considered that recommendations were more likely to be accepted if they were well argued and conclusions were clearly evidenced and that, prior to the Standards, this was an area of weakness in reports prepared by generic workers. The sheriffs and court social workers agreed that the majority of recommendations were adequately argued. Although some sheriffs thought that this aspect had improved as a result of the Standards, others thought that the standard of reports had been very high prior to policy implementation.

Most sheriffs said they would tend to follow the recommendation if it was realistic, arising from the body of the report and took into account the gravity of the offence. However, both sheriffs and social workers agreed that, as social workers did not have access to the evidence presented in court, their recommendation, based on the offender's version of the circumstances surrounding the offence, might then be quite unrealistic. In these circumstances, the recommendation might not be followed by the sheriff and might be seen as a plea in mitigation. The reality of these concerns has been demonstrated by other researchers. For example, Gelsthorpe and Raynor (1995) found that:

> "In many cases, definitions of unrealistic recommendations appeared to have as much to do with the tone of recommendations as with the actual content, so that what was unrealistic to a sentencer would easily become acceptable if framed within the context of reasoned discussion". (1995: p.196)

The importance of the wording of conclusions and recommendations was recognised by the social workers interviewed in our study. Some even indicated a reluctance to use the term "recommendation". This concern can be seen to be justified, as, although the majority of sheriffs said that they did not object to recommendations, one sheriff challenged the role of the SER recommendation:

> "At the end of day it's the sheriff who has to make up his mind not the social worker. It's not their job to balance the general interest of the public (fear and disenchantment of the public and to protect the public) against that of the accused. SERs are weighted in favour of the accused - a plea in mitigation". (Sheriff)

Influence of the Action Plan

Most sheriffs said that the absence of an action plan did not necessarily discourage them from imposing probation, although if there was an action plan and it was constructive and realistic, they might have been more likely to consider probation. Whilst some sheriffs were satisfied that, if there was a lack of detail in the plan, they would have confidence that the social worker would undertake the work required, other sheriffs would ask for a supplementary report to supply more details.

Time to Read Reports

The National Standards state that SERs should be submitted by noon on the day prior to the court. In one court (Burns) the sheriffs did not receive SERs until the morning of the court, although the majority were given to the sheriff clerk on the preceding afternoon. Both sheriffs and social workers noted that some temporary sheriffs did not tend to arrive in court more than ten minutes before the court was due to sit. If the sheriff had only a short time in which to read the SERs and court papers of the morning's cases, it is possible that the influence of the report might have been reduced.

Anticipating the Sheriff's Decision

All sheriffs considered that social workers should not take into account the interests and practices of individual sheriffs but should maintain their professional independence, although some sheriffs suggested that there might be an argument for it in a small court which had one resident sheriff and few temporary sheriffs. This latter view was not shared by the sheriff from the small court in the sample who said:

> "I would hope that the Standards will encourage a uniform provision of essential information before sentence and I don't see that it is right that the writer should table the report to the perceived sentencer because it is an independent report". (Sheriff)

Curran and Chambers (1982) found that there was a higher level of acceptance in rural areas or small towns as the sheriff may have had more frequent opportunities to inform social workers of what he expected from a report or that social workers felt under pressure to make recommendations which they considered the sheriff could accept. The social workers from the rural area in our study suggested that the sheriff did influence the content of their SERs as he frequently used to return reports for further information and was involved in training social workers in the preparation of SERs. However they said:

> "A sheriff like ours, by necessity, makes you become a far better report writer than someone who couldn't care what you write". (Social workers)

It was noted that in our sample the level of acceptance of recommendations in this court was relatively high compared to other courts in our sample. There is a danger that, if social workers are influenced too much by a sheriff, they may not necessarily work to the National Standards. The probation study (McIvor and Barry, 1998) found that this area was least likely to target probation on high risk offenders and was least likely to meet the Standards in relation to supervision.

The court social worker from Burns thought that social workers should "bear in mind" the interests and practices of individual sheriffs but this should not influence the substance of the report. However, social workers in most courts would not know which sheriff would read the report as there were several permanent sheriffs and many temporary sheriffs.

Although some social workers might have been able to anticipate the sheriff's decision, most indicated that they maintained their professional independence and recommended the disposal which, on the basis of their assessments, they considered was most appropriate. For example, social workers did not necessarily agree with the practice in some courts of imposing custody for certain offences such as carrying knives, as they considered that the most effective way to focus on that type of offending behaviour was to try to prevent a recurrence through intensive probation. In such cases, they would recommend probation which often resulted in their recommendation not being followed by the sheriff.

CONCLUSION

Examination of sentencing trends and levels of conversion of SER recommendation to disposal provide indicators of sentencing practice.

We have seen that the proportion of cases given custody in sheriff courts in Scotland and in the study courts had increased since 1991, contrary to the policy objectives. However the use of short custodial sentences had decreased and the use of probation had increased, especially in the under 21 age group in the study courts. These trends were consistent with policy projectives.

A discussion of the factors which might influence sentencing trends, identified those which were related to the policy, such as the delay in its full implementation and provision of feedback to sentencers on the effectiveness of community based disposals. Factors which were not related to the policy include the increase in incidence of crimes and offences which might attract a custodial sentence.

On the other hand, factors influencing conversion of SER recommendation to disposal were mainly found to be related to the policy, such as the content and presentation of information in SERs. However, the differing roles of the SER author and the sentencer, who has to consider wider issues such as the public interest, are likely to result in a certain level of discrepancy.

The final chapter explores the factors which influence sentencing decisions and the impact of the policy on these factors.

CHAPTER SIX
THE IMPACT OF THE POLICY ON SENTENCING DECISIONS

INTRODUCTION

It was agreed by the evaluation strategy working group (September 1990) that the objectives of the funding initiative are to:

- reduce the use of custody in the criminal justice system by increasing the availability, improving the quality and targeting the use of community based court disposals and throughcare services on those most at risk of custody, especially young adult repeat offenders;

- enable offenders to address their offending behaviour and make a successful adjustment to law abiding life.

From the Central Government perspective, in order to achieve these principal objectives a number of intermediate objectives must be met. Those relating to sentencer decision making are: to increase the credibility of community based disposals available to the court by ensuring that National Standards are met; to ensure that the needs of the court are met in terms of an adequate supply of community based disposals of the required quality; and to ensure liaison arrangements exist between the social work departments and the courts which are capable of meeting the courts' needs for social work services.

Other studies in the research programme address the objectives relating to the risk of re-offending, the needs of young adult offenders and quality of probation and throughcare services.

THE QUALITY AND CREDIBILITY OF COMMUNITY BASED DISPOSALS

Sheriffs, social workers and social work managers considered that the quality and credibility of probation had significantly improved since the introduction of the policy, whereas they recognised that the credibility of community service, for which National Standards were introduced in 1989, was high prior to the 1991 policy. However, although social work managers and court social workers believed that greater specialisation, training and the National Standards guidance had strengthened probation supervision, they acknowledged that further improvements could be made, such as a need to be more analytic rather than descriptive. This view was confirmed by McIvor and Barry (1998) who found that probation supervision in the four study areas did not fully meet the requirements of the National Standards.

The analysis of SERs and feedback from interviews with sheriffs showed that the quality of SERs played an important role in assisting sentencing decisions. Sheriffs generally considered that the quality of SERs was high but, in reports in our sample, gaps were found in the provision of key information which sheriffs sought in SERs. In addition, sheriffs indicated that the quality of SERs, in particular whether recommendations were realistic and conclusions were based on the body of the report, could influence their decision whether or not to follow the SER recommendation. It was found that the sample reports did not always provide the information and assessments identified as "essential contents" by the National Standards, although social workers queried the necessity to include information which they did not consider to be relevant. Nevertheless, court social workers and social work managers recognised that further improvements should be made to SERs.

The results of other research and interviews with sheriffs in this study acknowledge that detailed feedback of information to sentencers on effectiveness of new measures (such as the use of community disposals for "high risk" offenders), may be required before credibility of these measures can be achieved.

Thus, although it was recognised that further improvements could be made to the quality of SERs and probation, significant steps have been taken to achieve an increase in the quality and credibility of community based disposals.

AVAILABILITY OF COMMUNITY BASED DISPOSALS

Only a limited success had been achieved in increasing the range of specialist services. Most specialist services had been introduced in the study areas prior to or shortly after the introduction of the policy. Gaps in service provision relating to the range of specialist services and number of available places, were identified by social workers and some sheriffs. These sheriffs suggested that a lack of appropriate specialist services, such as

STAFFORDSHIRE
UNIVERSITY
LIBRARY

supervised and supported accommodation, could inhibit their use of community based disposals. However, sheriffs indicated that, in addition to the quality and availability of services, they considered the protection of the public, risk of re-offending and other factors relating to the individual, when deciding between custody and a community based disposal.

Some managers and social workers considered that the low or sometimes erratic demand for specialist services in rural areas precluded the development of locally based initiatives. This may have implications for the more rural new local authorities.

LIAISON

The policy objective of ensuring the existence of liaison arrangements which meet the court's needs was only partially achieved. Informal liaison was said by sheriffs and social workers to have operated well. However, some sheriffs identified a need for more detailed feedback on the outcome of community based disposals for "high risk" offenders. Formal liaison meetings should provide an opportunity for such feedback and an opportunity to discuss priorities for requesting SERs and gaps in service provision. However, some sheriffs were reluctant to attend formal meetings with senior social work management.

ORGANISATIONAL ARRANGEMENTS

Social work managers and court social workers considered that the preparation of SERs and probation supervision had improved partly as a result of increased specialisation, as social workers could develop their skills and expertise. However, the organisational changes undertaken as a result of policy implementation were radical in most areas and it is likely that these changes would require some time to settle before an improved quality of service could be achieved.

The study areas were selected to represent, amongst other factors, differing levels of specialisation in the organisation of service delivery. Social work managers (Brown, Levy and McIvor, 1998) reported that the authorities in which the greatest progress had been made in introducing more structured offence focused methods of probation work, were those which had the clearest specialist structures. Despite this, the study area where social workers' time was not wholly allocated to criminal justice work, was found, overall, to meet the National Standards most closely (McIvor and Barry, 1998).

CONCLUSION

We have seen that significant progress has been made towards policy implementation and that there was some evidence of success in achieving policy objectives, such as an increase in the use of probation and a reduction in the use of short custodial sentences. It is, however, important to recognise that, as sentencers consider other factors in addition to social work services, there is a limit to the extent to which social work policy can influence sentencing decisions.

Nevertheless, we noted that the National Standards had not been fully implemented, as the research fieldwork was undertaken in the early stages of policy implementation. It was recognised that, although service delivery is moving in the right direction, further improvements in service provision could be made to fully realise the potential of the social work contribution to sentencing decisions.

ANNEX I

NATIONAL STANDARDS: OBJECTIVES OF SOCIAL WORK PRACTICE IN THE CRIMINAL JUSTICE SYSTEM

1. To enable a reduction in the incidence of custody, whether on remand, at sentence, or in default of a financial penalty, where it is used for lack of a suitable, available community based social work disposal.

2. To promote and enhance the range and quality of community based social work disposals available to the courts and ensure that they are managed and supervised in such a manner that they have the confidence of courts, the police and the public at large.

3. To ensure that the social work disposals are provided to the courts or other agencies in such a way that the full range of disposals is available when required so that the most appropriate one can be used, particularly with persistent offenders.

4. To give priority to the development of community based social work disposals and other services to young adult offenders.

5. To promote the development of schemes to enable the courts to grant bail in an increased number of cases.

6. To provide and facilitate services for prisoners and their families, to help them prepare for release from custody and to assist them resettle in the community on release within the law.

7. To help offenders tackle their offending behaviour, assist them to live socially responsible lives within the law, and whenever appropriate, further their social integration through the involvement and support of their families, friends and other resources in their community.

8. To assist the families of offenders where family life suffers as a consequence of offending behaviour.

9. To promote, provide and facilitate the development of schemes for diverting accused persons from prosecution to social work in those cases where there is sufficient evidence to prosecute but it is not deemed necessary to do so in the public interest.

10. To promote and assist the development of services to the victims of crime.

11. To promote and assist action to reduce and prevent crime.

(National Standards 1991, part 1, paragraph 12.)

ANNEX II

METHODOLOGICAL ISSUES

Methods

This study examined the Scottish Office criminal justice statistics from 1989 to 1994 in one sheriff court from each of the four study sites and for all sheriff courts in Scotland. The courts were selected on the basis of sentencing patterns, the volume of charges proved and geographical location (to include courts serving both urban and rural locations). It should be noted that all four of the study courts had a medium to high use of custodial disposals. It may be that courts with this type of sentencing pattern have a stronger resistance to the policy objective of reducing the use of custody by increasing the use of community based disposals. For this reason, the impact of the policy on sentencing patterns may be less clear than had different courts been selected. However, there may also have been more potential to reduce the use of custodial disposals in these courts than in those where the use of custodial disposals was already low.

A sample of social enquiry reports was drawn from each of the four study courts. There were three purposes of recording the content of social enquiry reports: to identify issues to be raised in interviews; to consider the extent to which reports had covered information specified as "essential contents" in the National Standards; and to explore the relationships between characteristics of the case, the recommendation made and the sheriff's decision in court. The content of reports was therefore recorded using a pre-coded instrument designed by reference to the National Standards list of "essential contents". Any information which appeared regularly but was not required by the Standards was also recorded. Supplementary information about the nature of the offence was collected from police reports, details of the current conviction and disposal were obtained from court records and a list of previous convictions and disposals was obtained from The Scottish Criminal Records Office.

Factors influencing sentencer decision making were explored via semi-structured interviews with :

* seven sheriffs, all of whom were resident in the study areas[24];

* one representative of the Procurators Fiscal's Office at three of the study courts;

* one court social worker from each study court; and

* a group interview of four social workers from each court area who were involved in writing the social enquiry reports included in the samples.

---

[24] In Bruce and Burns, all of the resident sheriffs were interviewed. In Scott and Wallace, the larger courts, it was not feasible to interview all resident sheriffs. Two sheriffs were selected from each of these courts to represent the range of views of sheriffs in their court.

Selection of the social enquiry report sample

The social enquiry reports were selected on the basis of the recommendations made by the author. The intention was to sample the most recent reports in each of the study areas recommending : probation (20); community service (20); and deferred sentence with some form of social work service (10) as well as 10 reports which made no recommendation. This quota sample allowed the research to focus specifically on recommendations for services in which there was a policy interest as well as to investigate the reasons for and the impact of reports making no recommendation. The "no recommendation" sub-sample comprised reports in which the authors clearly stated that they were unable to offer a recommendation, and/or reports in which a range of disposals was presented but no preference was stated.

The deferred sentence sub-sample comprised recommendations that sentence be deferred either to allow the offender to continue to receive a service already being provided or to introduce some form of social work intervention. However, using these criteria it was not possible to obtain the full quota of these recommendations in any of the study courts. It seemed that this type of recommendation was rarely made because services offered in this context were not funded by central government. A total sample of 212 reports were obtained in the sample: probation (79); community service (79); deferred sentence (14); and no recommendation (40).

Depending upon the turnover of social enquiry reports in each of the study sites, reports were obtained via either a retrospective or a rolling sample. In Wallace, for example, where there was a high turnover of reports, it was possible to obtain them entirely on a rolling basis. However, in the remaining three sites the majority of reports were obtained retrospectively. Although sampling on a rolling basis meant that the research was guaranteed recent reports, it also meant that the authors of the reports may have been aware that their reports could be analysed.

It was also necessary to guard against another possible form of bias in the selection of reports for analysis. One method of identifying recent social enquiry reports for inclusion in the study would have been to search through active case files for reports prepared at the time of the court hearings. However, given that subjects would be receiving some form of social work service, it is very likely that these reports would have made a successful recommendation for a community based disposal. The correlation between recommendation and outcome in a sample obtained in this way would therefore be distorted.

Client confidentiality

In the interest of client confidentiality, it was originally intended that the subjects of social enquiry reports would be asked to register their consent to access by signing and returning a form. Aggregated data on the basic characteristics of clients who refused access would be obtained from the social work office in order to identify if there was any systematic bias in the sample who consented. However, when this procedure was piloted in one of the study sites, too few clients returned the forms to make the research feasible. It was therefore agreed that reports would instead be anonymised at the point of data collection. The research team also gave its assurance that data would be confidentially stored and that no one, other than the researchers, would have access to it.

Limitations of the sample

By virtue of the fact that a social enquiry report has been prepared, we can assume that many of the subjects included in the sample were regarded as being at risk of custody. Any sample of social enquiry reports is therefore likely to include a high proportion of relatively serious offences such as property crimes and crimes against the person. It is also likely to include a high proportion of young offenders because sentencers must request a social enquiry report before imposing a custodial sentence on offenders under the age of 21. It also follows that the type of disposals received by the subjects of social enquiry reports will not be typical of the overall sentencing pattern of that particular court. The samples should therefore not be viewed as representative of the total throughput of cases in those study courts, nor should they be viewed as necessarily being representative of the throughput of social enquiry reports at these study courts.

ANNEX III

SENTENCING TRENDS 1989-94

Table 1: Selected Disposals as Percentage of All Charges Proved (Sheriff Courts)[25]

	Scott %	Wallace %	Burns %	Bruce %	Scotland %
Custody					
1989	11	15	10	9	12
1990	12	14	9	7	12
1991	13	12	12	7	11
1992	16	15	12	14	13
1993	16	14	10	15	14
1994	18	17	10	12	15
Probation					
1989	6	2	4	4	4
1990	6	4	4	4	4
1991	6	7	5	6	5
1992	6	8	8	6	5
1993	8	9	7	7	6
1994	7	8	7	8	6
Community Service					
1989	3	8	7	4	5
1990	3	7	8	7	5
1991	5	6	11	6	6
1992	8	9	10	7	6
1993	6	8	9	5	6
1994	8	8	5	6	6
Fines					
1989	70	60	67	69	69
1990	69	61	67	68	68
1991	65	59	58	65	67
1992	59	56	52	64	64
1993	61	55	58	62	62
1994	58	53	53	62	61

---

[25] Percentages do not add up to 100 % as this table excludes "other" disposals, such as compensation and admonition.

Table 2: Selected Offences as a Proportion of All Crimes and Offences 1989- 1994

	Scott		Wallace		Burns		Bruce		Scotland	
	NO.	%	NO.	%	NO.	%	NO.	%	NO.	%
Theft of MV										
1989	131	3.0	52	1.6	52	2.0	14	1.1	2131	2.4
1990	105	2.6	68	2.4	44	1.6	20	1.9	2186	2.5
1991	116	3.6	57	2.4	35	1.4	26	2.5	2137	2.6
1992	153	4.5	84	2.8	39	1.7	14	1.4	2386	2.8
1993	178	5.0	105	3.6	35	1.7	11	1.1	2229	2.7
1994	171	4.3	95	3.1	29	1.5	14	1.5	2245	2.7
House-breaking										
1989	261	5.8	375	11.2	117	4.5	66	5.2	6211	6.9
1990	234	5.8	284	10.1	131	4.8	47	4.3	5890	6.8
1991	203	6.2	207	8.7	117	4.6	47	4.5	5281	6.5
1992	220	6.5	341	11.2	104	4.5	45	4.3	5541	6.5
1993	239	6.7	203	6.9	126	6.2	47	4.8	5026	6.2
1994	267	6.6	198	6.5	84	4.4	37	3.9	4877	5.9
Handling Weapons										
1989	103	2.3	38	1.1	21	0.8	16	1.3	864	1.0
1990	70	1.7	22	0.8	27	1.0	8	0.7	738	0.8
1991	56	1.7	22	0.9	22	0.9	15	1.4	730	0.9
1992	89	2.6	23	0.8	20	0.9	13	1.3	1200	1.4
1993	107	3.0	22	0.7	15	0.7	15	1.5	1402	1.7
1994	82	2.0	28	0.9	19	1.0	10	1.1	1398	1.7

Table 3: Use of Custody for Selected Offences 1989-1994

	Scott %	Wallace %	Burns %	Bruce %	Scotland %
Theft of MV					
1989	18	23	12	21	21
1990	29	16	7	15	22
1991	23	26	9	23	22
1992	24	32	21	36	26
1993	24	27	26	27	28
1994	33	28	28	14	30
Housebreaking					
1989	30	41	45	35	37
1990	28	43	35	32	35
1991	32	33	38	38	35
1992	38	37	37	38	37
1993	37	39	48	51	41
1994	40	45	36	43	44
Handling Weapons					
1989	13	11	29	-	17
1990	16	5	4	13	13
1991	11	9	-	-	12
1992	22	-	30	23	21
1993	28	18	33	20	23
1994	35	21	11	-	25

Table 4: Length of Custodial Sentence

	1989 %	1990 %	1991 %	1992 %	1993 %	1994 %
Scotland						
Up to 1 month	15	15	15	14	13	10
> 1 to 3 months	49	47	46	46	45	43
> 3 to 6 months	24	25	26	26	28	31
> 6 to 12 months	7	8	8	8	8	9
> 1 year +	5	5	5	5	6	7
Scott						
Up to 1 month	18	21	15	15	14	11
> 1 to 3 months	49	45	45	45	42	37
> 3 to 6 months	23	22	26	27	25	36
> 6 to 12 months	6	7	10	8	11	8
> 1 year +	4	5	4	5	8	7
Wallace						
Up to 1 month	32	30	34	24	23	16
> 1 to 3 months	50	46	38	50	49	46
> 3 to 6 months	15	18	23	19	22	25
> 6 to 12 months	1	4	4	5	4	8
> 1 year +	2	2	1	2	3	5
Burns						
Up to 1 month	14	13	13	19	14	13
> 1 to 3 months	46	45	51	50	46	41
> 3 to 6 months	29	30	26	24	28	32
> 6 to 12 months	7	7	5	5	6	8
> 1 year +	5	5	5	3	6	6
Bruce						
Up to 1 month	12	10	12	8	12	4
> 1 to 3 months	59	64	57	55	53	47
> 3 to 6 months	21	19	24	28	24	34
> 6 to 12 months	6	6	5	7	8	12
> 1 year +	2	-	2	2	2	2

REFERENCES

Brown, L., Levy, L. and McIvor, G. (1998). *Social Work and Criminal Justice: The National and Local Context.* Edinburgh: The Stationery Office.

Carter, R. M. and Wilkins, L. T. (1967). Some Factors in Sentencing Policy. *The Journal of Criminal Law, Criminology and Police Science*, 58, No. 4. 503-514.

Curran, J. H. and Chambers, G. A. (1982). *Social Enquiry Reports in Scotland.* A Scottish Office Social Research Study, Edinburgh: HMSO.

Ford, R., Ditton, J. and Laybourn, A. (1992). *Probation in Scotland: Access and practice.* Edinburgh: The Scottish Office Central Research Unit.

Gelsthorpe, L. and Raynor, P. (1995). Quality and Effectiveness in Probation Officers' Reports to Sentencers. *The British Journal of Criminology*, 35, No. 2, 188-200

McAra, L. (1998) *Social Work and Criminal Justice: Early Arrangements.* Edinburgh: The Stationery Office.

McAra, L. (1998a). *Social Work and Criminal Justice: Parole Board Decision Making.* Edinburgh: The Stationery Office.

McIvor, G. and Barry, M. (1998). *Social Work and Criminal Justice: Probation.* Edinburgh: The Stationery Office.

McIvor, G. and Barry, M. (1998a). *Social Work and Criminal Justice: Community Based Throughcare.* Edinburgh: The Stationery Office.

Paterson, F. and Tombs, J. (1998). *Social Work and Criminal Justice: The Impact of Policy.* Edinburgh: The Stationery Office.

Sabol, W. J. (1990). Improvement, Fines and Diverting Offenders from Custody: Implications of Sentencing Discretion for Penal Policy. *The Howard Journal*, 29, No. 1, 25-41.

Social Work Services Group (1991). *National Objectives and Standards for Social Work Services in the Criminal Justice System.* Edinburgh: The Scottish Office.

The Scottish Office Social Work Services Inspectorate (1996). *Helping the Court Decide: Report of an Inspection of Social Enquiry Reports for the Criminal Courts.* Edinburgh: The Scottish Office.

Printed in Scotland for The Stationery Office Limited
J37711, C7, 2/98, CCN 003808

04299085